BUILDING AND RACING

Radio Control
SAILBOATS

RC PERFORMANCE SERIES NO. 10

BY THOMAS J. HOULE

KALMBACH BOOKS

Designer: Sabine Beaupré

First printing, 1993. Second printing, 1994. Third printing, 1996

Library of Congress Cataloging-in-Publication Data

Houle, Thomas.
    Building and racing radio control sailboats / by Thomas Houle, Jr.
        p.   cm. -- (RC performance series ; no. 10)
      ISBN 0-89024-115-5
      1. Sailboats--Models--Radio control. I. Title. II. Series.
    VM359.H67 1993
    623.8'201--dc20   92-42787

CONTENTS

Fig. 1-1. Two AMYA Marblehead class boats match race to windward in a heavy blow. Exciting? You bet! The best part is you can do it too.

1

THE LURE OF RC SAILING

Sailboats are fascinating. Look at the number of people who stop and watch a full-size or model sailboat work its way quietly across a lake or pond. Many youngsters follow youthful instincts and build barks and brigantines out of cork hulls, toothpick masts, square-rigged paper sails or walnut shells. As a child filled with dreams of faraway places, I sailed my tiny galleons single-handedly to Zanzibar and beyond—all in my bathroom sink.

Years later, after a long stint in radio-controlled aircraft modeling, I was introduced to the art of radio-con-

trolled sailing. I was standing at a pond one day watching model boats sail by, when someone passed me a transmitter and asked me if I'd like to try it. My first thought was that the boat was going to capsize and I'd look like a first-class fool. As I guided it back and forth in front of me for a few minutes, (as I recall the boat didn't have sail control) I realized steering it was easy. It struck me how similar RC sailing was to sailing a real boat. The model was a little quicker, but it always did what I asked it to and in the same manner as a full-size boat.

Even though I wasn't in the boat

and couldn't feel or hear its response, it reminded me of the small dinghies I used to sail on the inland lakes. The boat would catch a puff, gently heel, and quickly accelerate. It made me want a boat of my own. This was a whole new world!

That first afternoon of RC sailing brought back many half-forgotten memories: days spent alone or with a friend in a small dinghy, muscles sore from hanging half in and half out of the boat in a delicate balancing act intended to keep the little boat on its feet. When I sailed my first RC boat, I knew nothing about building and racing RC sailboats, but I was hooked and eager to learn. The boat club I was watching that day had several members who were experienced model sailboat skippers. They guided me patiently through the beginner's maze of equipment and techniques. With their support, I was building and sailing my own boats in a short time. Racing came a little later.

WHO QUALIFIES?

Anyone can learn to build and sail just for the fun of it, and a beginner can graduate to organized racing in several different classes. In our club, we have active and retired full-size boat skippers, model aircraft and car drivers, and just plain beginners of all ages. A love of sailing is our common bond, and it's a never-ending set of challenges. I don't think anyone completely masters the art of building, sailing, and racing because there are always new products, techniques, racing tactics, and boat designs to try.

Joining a club is one of the most effective ways to get into this hobby. Some clubs (like mine) sponsor both sail and electric power while others are exclusively sail. Some clubs confine their racing to one class and others will have two or more active racing classes. In any case, the members can steer you through the learning process: where to buy components, rigging and hull planking, how to tune your boat, and so on—all the stuff you need to know to be a successful skipper.

EQUIPMENT

Unlike RC airplanes, sailboats don't crash! And they don't wear out generally. With corrective maintenance, they just keep on sailing year after year. While the startup expense can equal an RC airplane, the cost is spread over a much longer time frame, and most of the internal components will go from boat to boat before they wear out.

I'll discuss the boats and their sails later in the book and the sidebar in this chapter contains a list of tools you'll need. For now, though, I want to address radios, which are the second most important part to buy. Most often two-channel radios are used. Four or more channels are used by some skippers for options like adjustable backstay tension, jib twitcher, adjustable downhaul, and the like; but these functions are not needed or desirable for the beginner. Keep it simple and inexpensive when you start out.

Airtronic, Aristo-Craft, and Futaba manufacture inexpensive two-channel radios (you can find them for $50 to $75 at your local hobby shop or mail order firms). These radios are sold dry; that is, they are powered with AA-size dry cells. They are easily converted to rechargeable nicad batteries, but many people choose to stay with the inexpensive and reliable dry cells. The two-channel radio provides independent control of the rudder and sails, and transmitter range and receiver sensitivity are more than adequate (you'll lose sight of your boat before you'll lose control). The equipment is extremely reliable: dead batteries and a careless skipper are the most common failure modes.

This book is aimed at the beginner—the person who knows nothing about RC sailing or boat building. It will explain kits, scratchbuilding a boat, sails (where to buy them and tips on making your own), radio installation, sailboat racing rules and tactics, and building exact scale models that really sail. This book will get you started on a wonderful new hobby you can share for a lifetime with your family and friends.

Welcome aboard and fair winds!

Fig. 1-2. A scale model of the International One Design roars downwind. This model is 48 inches long and 72 inches tall from keel to masthead.

Fig. 1-3. The International One design sailing to windward.

Fig. 1-4. An AMYA U.S. One Meter class boat beating to windward. This boat, No. 457, is completely scratchbuilt.

Fig. 1-5. A completely scratchbuilt scale model: the John Alden design, Malabar Jr. It sails much like the real boat.

TOOLS YOU'LL NEED

HAND TOOLS

Screwdrivers. I keep an assortment ranging from a tiny jewelers' set up to a No. 2 Phillips and slotted head types. I also keep a few extra sizes in the kit I take to the pond.

Knives. A utility knife with a good supply of fresh blades will satisfy most cutting requirements. It will easily cut thin plywood, pine, and spruce—even mahogany. An X-Acto knife or equivalent with No.11 blades will do just about everything else.

Block plane. Small block plane really speeds up the smoothing out of rough planking. It can also fair plywood frames, stem pieces and spar cross-sections. Keep it sharp and make light cuts.

Scissors. An old pair of my wife's discarded sewing scissors is what I use for cutting sandpaper to fit my block sander, thin plywood, and fiberglass cloth.

Sanding block. An absolute must for sanding and shaping freshly planked hulls, decks, and spars. Don't even think of planking your hull without one. It should be at least 4-inches long. Pick one on which changing the sandpaper is easy; the easier it is the more likely you'll do it.

Sandpaper. You'll use all grades from very coarse 50 grit all the way up to super-fine 400-grit wet or dry on your fiberglassed hull. Use 400 grit and up sandpaper wet for best results (it'll last longer this way too).

Files. I use a 10-inch flat mill file for smoothing and shaping brass and aluminum fittings. Plus, it doesn't hurt to keep an inexpensive set of thin jewelers' files on hand for those lighter tasks.

Pliers. A pair of good slip-joints and long needle-nose pliers are about all I ever use. The long-noses are particularly useful for fishing broken sheets, trash and dropped nuts and bolts out of the hull. Keep an extra pair of each in the tool box you take to the pond.

Razor saw. An indispensable tool, I use one constantly while I'm building. There are several good brands available. I suggest you pick up the miter box that is usually available with the saw. It's he only tool worthy of cutting planking ends, spars and mahogany or teak trim.

Scriber. A hardened scriber point is especially useful for laying out hole centers and other outlines on sheet brass and aluminum. It's also used to spot holes before drilling them out.

Clamps. The more you have the better off you'll be. I keep a five-quart pail of wooden clothespins and light metal clamps handy on the bench. I use them throughout the building process for clamping al glue joints, including those made with CYA glue.

Metal shears. Some folks call them "tin snips." They're available in right-hand, left-hand and straight cut models. A straight pair will do for cutting out small fittings from brass and aluminum sheet stock.

Pin vise. I use one to drill the starter holes in the hull and spars for the myriad of metal fittings I put on my boats. The fittings are then attached with No. 1 and No. 2 brass RH wood screws. Get one with a palm pad; it saves the skin on the inside of your hand.

Small bowls. I keep all of our discarded margarine and butter tubs for mixing epoxy resin, paints, thinner. I typically go through several of these in the course of a single boat building project.

POWER TOOLS

Drill. A 1/4-inch chuck holeshooter will do. I use a 3/8-inch chuck with a variable speed trigger for my heavy drilling work. A hand-held motor tool such as those made by Dremel or Fordham are very useful. The drill press that is available from both of these firms is also useful for drilling out a series of brass fittings. You might also consider one of the small offshore table-top drill presses. These are sturdy enough to provide some semblance of routing ability.

Scroll saw. Useful for cutting out ply frames and shadows. If you buy one, get a good one. A cheap one with a wobbly blade that won't cut vertically isn't worth the grief it will bring.

Fig. 2-1. A trio of hulls showing the different hull shapes. The upper two models are exact scale designs; the bottom model with its long thin keel fin is an AMYA class U.S. One Meter.

2

SELECTING YOUR FIRST SAILBOAT

When selecting that first sailboat, you can choose from a wide variety of non-scale sport and racing designs or you can pick an exact or semi-scale model of your favorite prototype vessel.

The choice depends on your personal interest in boats. You may prefer the challenge of all-out racing without concern for authentic model design, or you may want to duplicate the real thing down to teak deck planking and brass fittings. You may elect to do some of both as well.

NON-SCALE CLASSES

The non-scale classes can be subdivided into two categories: one-design and open classes. One-design boats are built to a rigid set of rules: the hulls are produced in a common mold, spars and sails are identical, and nothing is left up to the builder. In the one-design classes, the objective is to pit

skipper against skipper, rather than boat against boat where hardware, building skill, and the amount of money invested may influence the outcome.

There are many one-design boats available in easy-to-build kit form. They come complete with a finished hull, deck, sails, and spars and require little assembly.

The Kyosho Fairwind is an excellent example of a smooth-sailing one-design that any beginner could handle with ease. They have been well tested over the years and several clubs race them as a club one-design. For all-out high performance racing, the Infinity 54 from the Amen Design Group (San Diego) is another excellent choice. Several clubs around the country race this boat.

In the open classes, experimentation and innovation are the order of the day. New hardware, exotic materi-

als, construction methods, weight-saving techniques, and the like are permitted and encouraged. The overriding goal is to build the fastest boat on the pond yet stay within the rules.

There are three fast-growing open classes: Marblehead, U. S. One Meter, and 36/600. These and several other racing classes are administered by the American Model Yachting Association (AMYA). Hull length, sail area, keel depth, and other details are controlled in the open classes. The rules are deliberately kept loose in order to spawn new designs and techniques.

Over the years, this has resulted in open-class boat designs that are extremely fast and great fun to sail in all wind conditions. On the other hand, to be competitive in some of these classes, you may have to spend quite a bit of money for the go-fast, high-tech hardware that the class may be using to maintain a competitive

Fig. 2-2. A scale model international One Design (foreground) and an AMYA U.S. One Meter class boat. The boats are close in size, but the non-scale U.S. One Meter is much faster.

Fig. 2-3. For all-out speed in any kind of weather, the AMYA Marblehead racing class is hard to beat. Length is 50 inches, and sail area is 800-square inches. An outstanding class, it's the largest single AMYA class.

edge. A tricked-out Marblehead class boat, for example, can run well over $500, and that does not include the radio. At the other extreme, there are used ready-to-sail U. S. One Meter boats available for less than $100; you will have to add a two-channel radio.

The Kyosho Fairwind one-design may not keep up with some of the open classes, but the Infinity 54 and Santa Barbara one-designs are very fast and would do well against the open classes. This is a moot point, however, since one-design boats usually would be raced only with other boats of the same class. So, for all skippers, especially beginners, the one-designs will provide as much racing excitement and challenge as any of the open classes. One-design boats are an excellent way for a club to break into racing.

AMYA (American Model Yachting Association) classes. The AMYA administers most of the organized racing events in this country. They also coordinate international events and class regulation with their European counterpart, the International Model Yacht Racing Union (IMYRU). The AMYA's basic goal is organized sailboat racing at the local, regional, and national level.

The AMYA maintains an active registry of all boats for each class, assigns class registration numbers, and monitors new class development. They will recognize a new class when twenty or more boats have been registered.

Several clubs race the Kyosho Fairwind and its predecessor, Tradewind one-designs. Neither of these is a registered AMYA class; but they are easy to assemble, and the beginner will learn an awful lot about sailing basics. They are very easy to sail; beginners can push them to their limits and make all kinds of mistakes, and neither boat will bite the hand that sails it.

There are currently fifteen registered AMYA classes, each controlled by a class secretary. This person coordinates the national regattas, registers new boats and assigns registration numbers, maintains the class rules, and, in general, toots a horn for that class. Each secretary is elected by the members of that class.

All AMYA classes are meant to go fast and turn quickly. In most classes, the hulls and spars are extremely light. The design goal is absolute minimum weight above the waterline. Typically, these boats are sensitive to rudder inputs and are very stiff—that is, they will not lay over easily in a strong breeze. Their turning radius is within a hull length or two.

This stiffness is a result of the exag-gerated depth of their keels, which is much deeper than you'd see on a scale model, and the sails tend to have very high aspect ratios (tall and thin plan forms). You will note the resemblance to a glider wing that is stood on its root chord. These two features make these boats very efficient to windward and much faster on a run than their scale cousins.

They can be sailed in winds up to 25 miles per hour, although even the most skilled skipper will have his hands full in these winds. At the other end of the spectrum, the tall, efficient sail plans generate enough lift to drive the boat in even the slightest breezes. They can be sailed and steered in glassy-smooth water.

There are plenty of exotic cottage industry, after-market components available for the racing classes: super light, carbon fiber masts, booms, and fin keels; Kevlar hulls; Dacron and Mylar sails; stainless steel fittings; and high-output, lightweight sail winches. Some classes have developed to such an extent that you may not be competitive if you are not willing to buy the required go-fast optional items.

Other classes. At the same time, other classes have been created for the skipper who wants to build his own hull, spars, and sails. The U. S. One

Fig. 2-4. The boat on the left is a Victor Soling. Available in kit form, it's an excellent beginner's racing boat. The other boat is a U.S. One Meter "Squirt."

Fig. 2-5. A 48-inch model of the Phil Rhodes ketch, "Dogstar" beats to windward in a moderate sea. All three sails are winch-controlled. The model is fast to windward.

Meter class is a good example, but there are others, too. The One Meter is an easy-to-build, inexpensive class for both beginners and experienced skippers. Performance is outstanding on all points of sail and in all types of weather. The overall hull length is 39-3/8 inches and the total sail area is 600 square inches. Mast heights range from 55 inches to 65 inches.

The U. S. One Meter class is an open class. Hulls are built from any material: wood, fiberglass, Kevlar, and even vacuum-formed plastic. Some skippers make their sails, others purchase them. It's a class where home-made boats can be as competitive as custom-built hulls.

Several years ago, the Ozaukee Model Shipwrights chose the U. S. One Meter class to race in biweekly regattas throughout the summer. To speed the building process and get to racing, the club assigned the various boat components to members who could handle the work most easily. Full-size sail patterns were drawn on a cadcam system and copies given to each member. One member poured a dozen lead keel bulbs. Another built the building boards. Another member cut pine and balsa stripwood. And so it went. In the end, the club had twelve kits to distribute to participating members. Within two months, the first boat was launched. Others took a year

or more to finish, but eventually all were built. (This is an important point for clubs that use this method. They will need to remember that each builder works at his own pace; it's a hobby, not a job).

The club estimated the average cost of each finished boat, including sails, to be around $40. Boat-to-boat performance has been comparable and outstanding. What a thrill for each member as, one by one, the boats were launched!

Sport or hobby? Time or money—the choice is yours. The higher the purchase cost, the less work you'll have to do in your workshop. It boils down to your perception of sailboat racing. Is it a sport or a hobby? If it's a sport for you, shelling out $500 or more may not be a problem. If it's a hobby, you may prefer to organize the work like the Ozaukee Model Shipwrights and enjoy the savings. You'll learn the basics of sailboat construction along with the black art of sailmaking. Either way, racing is exciting, fun, and competitive.

The AMYA is an outstanding source of how-to information on new boat designs, components, hulls, sails, and class rules as well as the latest scoop on who-beat-who at what regatta. The AMYA will also register your boat and make sure that all boats entered in AMYA-sponsored regattas meet the

class rules. The association's basic philosophy is that skipper skill should always be the ultimate factor in deciding the outcome of a race. The quarterly magazine, Model Yachting, is worth the annual membership fee. For membership information, write to:

Patricia Hein
AMYA Membership, secretary
1884 Campus Court
Rochester Hills, MI 48309

SCALE MODELS

Scale boats will usually be slower than their AMYA class counterparts. But for some hobbyists, boat speed is not the only measure of a model's worth. Many thrive on the excitement of racing while others enjoy researching, building, and sailing exact scale recreations of all sorts of racing, cruising, and cargo vessels from all eras.

It's very satisfying to watch a scale boat putter along in a light breeze. And it's very challenging to keep one of these boats on its feet in heavy air. Performance can be light years away from the AMYA classes because they are slower, sometimes ponderous, slow to respond to the rudder, and tender in a good breeze. Scale boats just won't be driven as hard as the AMYA boats and it takes a lot of skill to sail these boats well. In high winds they will demand all your attention. Their beauty lies in their scaled-down outlines

Fig. 2-6. A 40-inch model of the John Alden design, Malabar Jr. flies downwind. You can build just about any scale model and get reasonable handling and performance.

Fig. 2-7. Three Marbleheads, two on port tack, the other on starboard tack, work their way upwind to the first mark. Model sailboat racing is an exciting sport!

and performance in miniature.

From my perspective, I'll never have the chance to compare the performance of a full-size John Alden Malabar sloop to a Phil Rhodes ketch (two of my favorite designs); but having built and sailed exact scale replicas of them, I know now the relative performance differences between them. An accurately scaled model will replicate most of the original boat's performance characteristics. I can compare the performance of two different designs much like a naval architect would do in his test tank. The only difference is I do it on my pond.

For the racing afficionados, scale boats can be raced. There is a club in New York that races the Friendship Sloop as a one-design; all boats are built from the same Laughing Whale kit. The Ozaukee Model Shipwrights are studying the feasibility of racing a 48-inch LOA version of the International One-Design, a trim 1930s racing sloop from the waters of Long Island Sound. The class may still be raced actively there. The club has the female hull mold finished, and two hulls have been pulled so far to evaluate performance.

Due to car constraints and narrow basement landings, the most popular hull lengths are 36 inches to 50 inches. Extremes run from 30 inches to 80 inches LOA. Mast heights range from around 60 inches for a 36-inch hull, to 96 inches for a 72-inch hull. Masts always are made removable for transport and maintenance. (The largest boat that I can fit into my mid-size station wagon without disassembly is 48 inches long with a 62-inch mast.)

A 36-inch boat will weigh from 7 to 9 pounds. A 72-inch boat will range from 25 pounds to perhaps 65 pounds. Larger boats are harder to launch and retrieve; but because of their greater weight and mass, they are easier to sail and far less fidgety than the smaller boats, particularly in heavy air.

BOAT CLUBS

If there is a club nearby, by all means join it. Members can tell you what is being sailed locally and can guide you to the sources you'll need to get started. They will also check your RC gear before your maiden sail to ensure all the equipment is in working order. And they already should have a pond for you to sail on, complete with racing buoys.

So there you have it: racing or scale, it's up to you. If you can't decide, that's all right. There are plenty of avenues to explore in both areas. If you are at all interested in RC sailing you are bound to find something that appeals to you.

Fig. 3-1. The Robbe Rainbow No. 1056 kit is only 20 inches long. It's perfect for sailing in your swimming pool.

Fig. 3-2. Robbe's Comtess No. 1072 features a molded hull. It's 38 inches long and 59 inches high.

Fig. 3-3. Robbe's Koh-i-noor motor sailer No. 1126 is a scale model 40 inches long. It features an auxiliary drive motor, which is useful when the wind dies.

3

KITS WILL GET YOU STARTED

Kits win hands down as the fastest and easiest way for beginners to enter the world of radio-control sailing. Many questions asked by novices are answered by simply following the instructions that come with the kit. Terminology, for example, can be a big problem. Even those with considerable experience using gas and electric power boats will need to develop a new vocabulary, learn different building techniques, and use hardware they may have never seen before. There are a variety of unique fittings, lines, and other devices that can cause problems for the newcomer—not to mention having to learn a whole new language (figure 3-12, page 12).

Some skippers who have been sailing for years still don't use or understand sailboat terminology. Such terms as luff, jibe, gooseneck, halyard, and many more are still a mystery. However, building a kit will acquaint you with the traditional, albeit peculiar, language of sailing .

Kit plans and instruction manuals will guide you through the building process by using the correct terminology and corresponding illustrations. Sailing lingo is a sort of nautical shorthand; it allows you, for example, to refer to the sail "luff" rather than the "leading edge or front of the sail." Or, instead of saying "I turned the boat through the eye of the wind as I sailed downwind," you simply say, "I jibed" (see glossary, page 62).

CONSTRUCTION METHODS

You will learn many new construction methods as you progress through your first kit. Usually, if the hull is planked, the frames will be sawn or die cut for you. Also, the frames will be faired and true so that you won't have to fair them up to get a smoothly planked hull. The kit instructions will show you how to erect the frames to ensure a straight

hull. There may be photos and drawings to show the planking sequence.

Planking a hull is not terribly difficult, but having step-by-step instructions helps when you are doing it for the first time. If you prefer fiberglass or plastic, there are other kits available. You will, of course, pay more for these; but they offer a real saving in construction time. These kits may include a plastic or fiberglass deck as well. Since most of the wood parts are cut out for you, hull and spar construction will move right along. Completely sewn and ready-to-use sails usually are included in the kit. Some kits do not include the sails, but both custom and standard suits of sails are available from any of several commercial sailmakers. Unless you have a friend who has made a set of sails, I strongly suggest that you use the sails that come with the kit or buy a commercial suit. For the uninitiated, sailmaking can be difficult and frus-

Fig. 3-4. Robbe's Skandia No. 1075 is a semi-scale boat 40 inches long. It takes two channels: rudder and sails.

Fig. 3-5. The Robbe Topas No. 1012 is a semi-scale model of a European ketch. It's 41 inches long and takes two channels.

Fig. 3-6. Robbe's Topcat No. 1015 will satisfy avid multi-hull enthusiasts. It's 54 inches long, 86 inches high.

trating. If you are adventurous, go ahead. But don't be surprised if you have unexpected wrinkles and bags in your first suit (which may be just the incentive needed to build a second and better set).

Running and stayed rigging also can be mystifying for the beginner. Running rigging means lines that move when the boat is under sail; stayed rigging is permanent and does not move. Virtually all running and stayed rigging lines are made to be adjustable. Routings can get quite complex as well, especially when you start to run the lines and try to make sure they don't get caught or snagged. The kit instructions will steer you through this maze. Once you have done it, you'll see that it's not that complicated. It's that first time with no outside help that can really get to you. This is where joining a club can be a real asset.

All sailboats need substantial weight below the waterline to keep them on their feet when going to wind-

Fig. 3-7. The Robbe flagship is their Atlantis No. 1130, a scale model of a 92-foot schooner. The model is 55 inches long. It's an impressive sight at the pond.

Fig. 3-8. Another shot of the Robbe Atlantis. Optional features include wood deck planking and Genoa sail set.

Fig. 3-9. The Dumas sailboat kit lineup. From the left: Twelve Meter kit No.1111, Bingo kit No. 1108, Echells 22 No. 1109, and the Equation kit 1106. Write for its catalog or visit a hobby shop.

ward, and lead is the preferred material for this job. It may be stowed permanently in the bottom of the hull (the bilges) or, better yet, it can be suspended under the hull like a real sailboat. The deeper the lead is placed, the more effective it becomes and the less is required to do the same job. It's a good example of the simple lever: the lead acts as a counterforce to the lifting pressure of the sails. This heeling force is most pronounced when the boat is sailing to windward.

Depending on the kit, either molded lead or a mixture of lead birdshot and epoxy is used for the keel weight. In a given volume, solid lead weighs more than birdshot and epoxy; but birdshot is a lot easier to pour and retain with epoxy. Melting and pouring lead into a mold is a difficult and dangerous process which the kit manufacturer has taken care of for you. Sometimes the molded lead keel is purchased separately; it should be available in the shape and weight your kit needs.

To check out current kit availability, visit your local hobby shop and check the ads in the model boat magazines. There are a number of smaller kit manufacturers that distribute through the mail, while others sell through both the hobby shops and by

Fig. 3-10. The Victor Manufacturing Soling kit. It meets AMYA U.S. One Meter class requirements and is easy to build and sail. Some clubs use this design as their racing class.

Fig. 3-11. Two of Pop-Up Manufacturing's kits, the Pop-Up Catamaran and the AMYA U.S. 12 Meter class. The catamaran's hull is 48 inches long. It features a self-righting mechanism in case you flip the boat.

mail.

Along with the boat kit, you will also need a two-channel radio and a sail winch. Some of the kits will sail without the use of a winch; the Kyosho Tradewind and Fairwind are examples. But if you want to do anything more than just steer your boat around the pond you will definitely need a winch. Start out with one and get used to using it. Radio and winch installation are covered in detail in Chapters 5 and 7, respectively.

KIT TYPES AND MANUFACTURERS

Complete and short kits are available. Short kits are incomplete.

They usually include the hull, lead keel, rudder, and sometimes the deck; but the builder must purchase sails, spars, and hardware separately, often from the same firm. This process allows the builder to custom fit components from several manufacturers as he sees fit.

A list of complete and short kit firms follows. This list is by no means absolute. Due to the cottage industry nature of many of these firms, at any given time some are phasing out while others are phasing in.

The AMYA also is an excellent source of kit manufacturer ads and reference material, particularly for short kits and components that go

with them. The following is a list of some of the manufacturers that offer good kits.

Amen Design Group
(Complete kits,
sails, and components)
929 West St.
Petaluma, CA 94952

Black Sails
(Components and sails)
4761 Niagara Ave.
San Diego, CA 92107

Bob's Boatyard
(Components and sails)
3785 Edinburg St.
Burnaby, British Columbia
V5C1R4

Boris Wereszczynski
(Sails)
143 Kingslake Rd.
Willowdale, Ontario M2J3G2

Dumas Products, Inc.
(Complete kits
and components)
909-G East 17th St.
Tucson, AZ 85719

Elmaleh Yachts
(Complete kits and
components)
661 Greenpoint Ave.
Brooklyn, NY 11222

Pop Up Mfg.
(Complete kits and
components)
27 Emerson Ave.
Amityville, NY 11701

Robbe Model Sport
(Complete kits and components)
180 Township Line Rd.
Belle Mead, NJ 08502

Victor Model Products
(Complete kits and components)
12258-1/2 Woodruff Ave.
Downey, CA 90241

Try a kit. They have been thoroughly tested and de-bugged before marketing and they are an excellent way into RC sailing. Robbe manufactures a broad selection of high quality, semi-scale boat kits including a schooner that handles and sails well. Their catamaran is also interesting.

The Victor kits are simple to build and inexpensive. They are good racing subjects. These kits feature molded plastic hulls and ready-to-use sails.

Dumas kits have either fiberglass or wood hull construction. Both types build and sail well. They also manufacture several sail winches for use in larger boats.

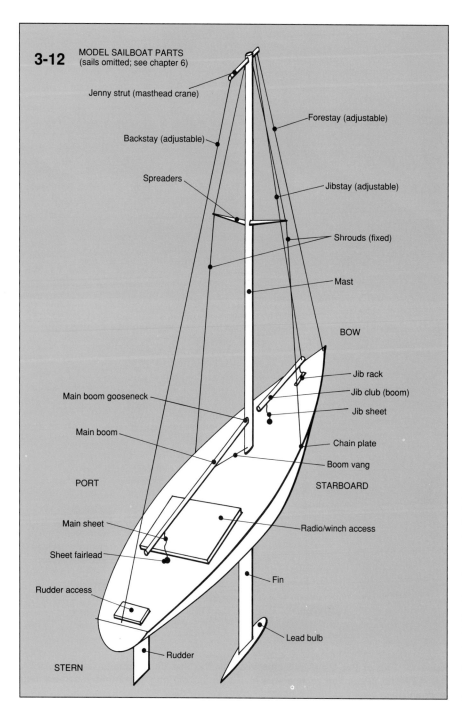

3-12 MODEL SAILBOAT PARTS
(sails omitted; see chapter 6)

Jenny strut (masthead crane)

Forestay (adjustable)

Backstay (adjustable)

Spreaders

Jibstay (adjustable)

Shrouds (fixed)

Mast

BOW

Jib rack

Jib club (boom)

Jib sheet

Main boom gooseneck

Main boom

Chain plate

Boom vang

PORT

STARBOARD

Main sheet

Radio/winch access

Sheet fairlead

Rudder access

Fin

Lead bulb

Rudder

STERN

Fig. 4-1A. 1/8-inch plywood shadows erected for an AMYA U.S. One Meter class hull. The shadows with cutouts will be left in the hull.

4

SCRATCHBUILDING

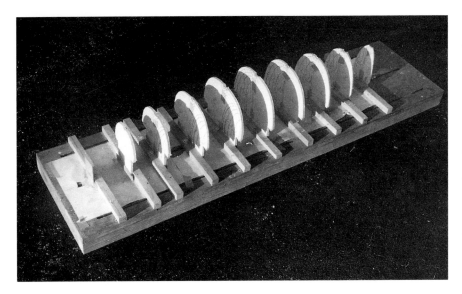

Fig. 4-1B. 3/16-inch foamboard works well for shadows. It accepts pins and is strong.

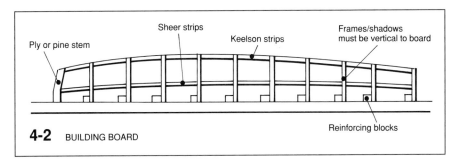

4-2 BUILDING BOARD

You might ask, why would anyone want to scratchbuild a sailboat with all those beautiful kits available? Well, for openers, it may be the only way to get the boat the way you really want it. Kit manufacturers can't possibly satisfy everyone's personal preferences.

Scratchbuilding, too, will allow you to try a variety of new materials. The club I belong to has several members who are constantly trying out new materials, processes, and structural techniques in an effort to build a lighter, faster, cheaper, or stronger boat. You can use soft woods, hardwoods, balsa, plastics, fiberglass, and epoxy or polyester resin. Or you can experiment with combinations of these materials. Even paper-mache molded over or in a form has been suggested as a good building medium. The point is, there are all kinds of materials at your local hobby shop and hardware store from which you can build a boat.

If you don't mind expending your own labor, scratchbuilding can save you a lot of money. There are plenty of inexpensive components that can be put to good use; for example, RC aircraft rudder horns, aileron bellcranks, ball link assemblies, small woodscrews, brass and aluminum strip and tubing, eyelets, Stryrene sheet and strip, hardwood veneers, and so on.

Regardless of your personal tastes in boats, there are thousands of model plans and full-size boat drawings available to the dedicated seeker of source materials. I spend a good deal of my time searching through secondhand bookstores, boating magazines such as *Woodenboat*, library book sales, and old model magazines. The Smithsonian has beautifully detailed drawings available for a great variety of American sailboats. You can write to them for a list and prices at: Smithsonian Institution, National Museum of American History, Division of Transportation, Rm. 5010, Washington, DC 20560.

There are also several American and British model boat magazines that feature monthly construction articles. Plans are usually available from the publisher.

Over time, I have developed a respectable library of "future projects." Frankly, I doubt I will ever get to all of them, but it was fun finding them. When I pick my next project I can choose from an awful lot of good stuff.

The AMYA is an excellent source of non-scale racing boat plans in various classes, boat building techniques, and sailmaking and trimming information. Their address is given in Chapter 2. I suggest you join. Even with their focus on racing, there is a lot of other infor-

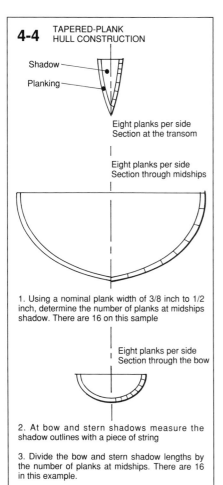

4-4 TAPERED-PLANK HULL CONSTRUCTION

Shadow

Planking

Eight planks per side
Section at the transom

Eight planks per side
Section through midships

1. Using a nominal plank width of 3/8 inch to 1/2 inch, determine the number of planks at midships shadow. There are 16 on this sample

Eight planks per side
Section through the bow

2. At bow and stern shadows measure the shadow outlines with a piece of string

3. Divide the bow and stern shadow lengths by the number of planks at midships. There are 16 in this example.

4. Taper each plank at the ends to these dimensions.

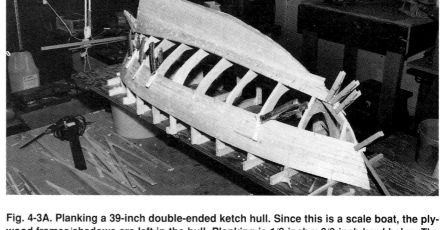

Fig. 4-3A. Planking a 39-inch double-ended ketch hull. Since this is a scale boat, the plywood frames/shadows are left in the hull. Planking is 1/8-inch x 3/8-inch hard balsa. The stem is 1/4-inch pine.

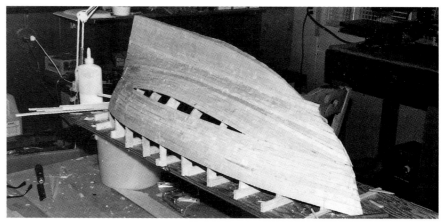

Fig. 4-3B. Here the planking is almost finished. There are lots of uneven planks and glue bumps. Figure 4-3C shows you how to clean these up.

mation that you as a scratchbuilder can use.

ENLARGING AN ORIGINAL DRAWING

Let's say you've found that boat you've always wanted to build, but all you have to work from is a tiny drawing. No problem. You can enlarge it to any size you want as long as you have side and top views along with the frame or station lines.

The original doesn't have to be perfectly accurate. The lines can be smoothed on the enlarged drawing. A sail plan also will have to be drawn; but this can be enlarged with the hull, or it can be easily scaled up separately using a ruler and protractor to duplicate the lines and angles.

The easiest (but most expensive) way is to have your local printer or graphics arts firm blow up the plan for you. Depending on the size of the blowup, this can really dent your wallet. Photocopiers can be used to enlarge frames and even hulls if done in several pieces.

A professionally drawn plan is not needed. It only has to be accurate enough to build a close copy of the

original. I have successfully used photocopiers and projectors (overhead, 35 millimeter, and opaque) to enlarge my drawings. In all cases the projector must be placed exactly at right angles to the wall onto which you are projecting the drawing. Failure to do so will result in a distorted projection.

If you shoot a 35-millimeter slide or a black-and-white negative, be sure the camera is set and locked so that it is perpendicular to the material to be copied. A copy stand with a bubble level is best for this kind of shot, although I have done it by taping the original to the wall and shooting the picture with a tripod-mounted camera. Both slide and black-and-white film will work, but I prefer the black-and-white. It seems to project an image with more contrast on the wall.

When I have the drawing squarely projected onto the wall, I tape a large sheet of paper over it. Then I trace the projected lines onto the paper. The only place I use a ruler is on the frame centerlines to provide an accurate common centerline for all the frames.

The beauty of this method is that the projector can be moved back and forth until I get the exact size hull I want. I can try several different sizes to see what is best. The sail plan and mast height also can be easily viewed and studied before any wood or sail material are cut.

My experience has been that for scale boats, a scale of 1 to 1-1/2 inches to the foot is a good starting point. This scale range typically will yield a model with a 36-inch to 50-inch hull—about right for the average car. I can just fit a 48-inch hull crosswise in the rear of my station wagon without having to remove the mast.

PLANKED WOOD HULL CONSTRUCTION

Erecting frames. The first step in hull construction is to erect a set of frames on a dead straight building board. These frames can be temporary or permanent. AMYA racing class boats usually will use temporary frames (called shadows) whereas scale boats will typically use permanent

Fig. 4-3C. Sand and fill the hull after planking. (see sidebar to the right on how to do this). When the balsa planking has been planed, sanded, and filled, the balsa skin is covered with fiberglass cloth. Six-ounce cloth was used on this hull.

Fig. 4-3D. Brush epoxy resin (thinned to the consistency of water) through the cloth. Three sanded coats should fill the cloth weave. Use auto body fillers to fill low spots before and after spraying on the prime coats.

Steps in sanding and filling the hull after planking is completed (the general techniques can be applied to most other sanding and filling jobs as well)

1. Sand the hull across the planks with a sanding block loaded with 50-grit sandpaper. The initial goal is to remove high spots and glue residue.
2. Lightly sand the hull lengthwise with the same sandpaper to clean up the keelson, stem, and transom areas.
3. Switch to 80 then 120-grit paper, working up to 220 grit. Always use a sanding block.
4. When the hull is fair and smooth, fill all cracks and low spots with a vinyl filler and fair into the hull with 220-grit sandpaper.
5. Add the pine bow piece, if there is one. Fair it in. The hull is now ready for fiberglassing.
6. A final sighting down the hull from several angles will reveal those last few pesky imperfections before the fiberglasss is applied.

frames. The temporary frames are used to save weight. To be competitive, the racing hulls need to be built as light as possible; and considering the way these hulls are planked and fiberglassed, the frames are not necessary anyway.

Occasionally the designer will specify leaving one or two frames in the midships area to support the radio and sail winch installation. In all cases, if available, follow the designer's instructions.

Due to their relatively large displacements, scale models will benefit by having their frames integrated right into the hull. Floating these hulls at their design waterlines will typically require twice the ballast of their non-scale racing counterparts. When adding ballast, keep it as low as possible in the hull. Relative to racing hulls, the scale boats tend to have high centers of gravity and keels that are not as deep as their racing sisters. This can cause excessive heeling in heavy air.

Racing hull shadows erected on a building board are shown in figures 4-1A and 4-1B. These hulls are AMYA U. S. One Meter class boats. Hull length is 39-3/8 inches. Since weight is not a factor, you can cut shadows from just about any material you have on hand. I use 3/16-inch-thick foam board for boats up to 65 inches in length. Others prefer to use 1/8-inch plywood. I like the foam board because of its ready ability to accept pins. (Pushing pins into plywood is not how I like to spend my weekends!) Foam board is available at art supply stores in 30-inch by 40-inch sheets in several thicknesses.

A typical AMYA racing hull will have ten shadows on equidistant centers. Erect the shadows vertically on the building board as shown in figure 4-2. Cut the stem and the transom from plywood.

To simplify hull construction, scale models should replicate the frame spacing of the full-size counterpart. I have done this on all my scale boats,

and each hull has faired out beautifully. Your scale boat, depending on its original designer, might have anywhere from 10 to 20 frames. Regardless of the number, erect the frames the same way as the racing hull — vertically and on scale centers. Stems can be cut and shaped from pine or spruce. Transoms can be cut from plywood.

For permanently installed frames, 1/8-inch to 1/4-inch ply will work well. Inexpensive poplar (light) ply or 1/8-inch doorskins can be used. Trim all frames so most of the inside of the frame is cut away to make room for the radio board and sail winch arm travel. Finished frames need not be more than 3/4-inch wide.

Cutting the ply frames is easy. Make photocopies of each frame, and rubber cement the patterns to the frame stock. Incidentally, this also will maximize the usage of your plywood stock. Cut them out on a jig or band saw and sand down to the outlines. Sheer and keelson notches are also cut at this point.

The frames should be erected on a building board that is dead straight (no twists). One-half-inch to 3/4-inch ply or particle board somewhat longer than your hull will do the job here. A straight piece of 2 by 4 also will work. Clamped in a vise, it gets the project up where it's comfortable to work on. Small blocks glued to the building board will reinforce the frame-to-board joints and ensure that the frames are vertical. All frames should be checked with a small square before the planking process is started.

The sheer clamps and keelson provide longitudinal strength to the hull

Fig. 4-3E. After the final coat of primer is sprayed on, lightly mark the waterline. (The easiest way to do this is with the hull still attached to the building board.) I use a wood block with a pencil hole drilled at the correct height.

Fig. 4-3F. The hull cut from the building board. Note the hull cradle: a simple plywood structure and the masking tape which marks the waterline. It's a good idea after the hull is removed from the building board to add a couple of temporary cross-braces until the permanent deck beams are installed.

skeleton. If you are building a racing hull, to facilitate removal of the shadows you will have to cover them with some kind of glue-resistant material before the sheers or keelson can be added. I like to use kitchen plastic wrap. It's transparent and resists just about all glues, including the CYA types.

The sheer clamp strips and the keelson strips are laminated 1/8-inch by 1/4-inch by 3/8-inch clear pine or spruce. Two laminations are usually sufficient for hulls up to 6 feet in length. Size is not that fussy; use what you have, but don't get carried away if you are trying to build a lightweight fast boat. When putting in these strips, the important thing is to check their fairness from stem to stern. There is nothing like getting down and simply eyeballing these curves; the humps and valleys are easy to spot. Shim and trim the frame notches as necessary to get smooth, fair curves. After the sheers and keelson are installed and faired, sand or plane the edges of the sheers so that they fair smoothly into each frame, the stem piece, and the transom.

Planking a hull. There are a couple of ways to plank a hull. The AMYA racing classes typically use balsa strip planking covered with fiberglass cloth and resin. The fiberglass cloth weight can range from 3/4 ounces to six ounces in weight depending on hull size. The U.S. One Meter class at 39-3/8-inch length doesn't need more than 3/4-ounce cloth, while a 6-foot boat would require one or two layers of 6-ounce cloth.

Medium-hard 5/16-inch to 3/8-inch-wide pieces stripped from 4-inch by 48-inch balsa sheets is the most economical way to go, but other woods can be used as well. Thin strips of mahogany veneer, willow, basswood,

Fig. 4-3G. Here's how the same ketch hull looks inside. The frames are cut from 3/16-inch poplar plywood. They are in the same locations as the full-size boat.

Fig. 4-3H. he deck framing complete. The sub-deck is 1/8 inch balsa and will be covered with 1/32-inch mahogany strips to simulate a planked deck. If the deck won't be veneered, 1/32-inch or 1/16-inch plywood can be used.

or just about anything will work provided you don't add too much weight. To save weight, apply thin veneers over a balsa shell. Clear varnished, they provide a beautiful hull. Figures 4-3A to 4-3K illustrate the complete hull building sequence. The same techniques apply to a racing hull.

Tapered-width plank hull. The planking can be constant or tapered width. Tapered planks eliminate the cutting and fitting of individual planks to the hull. If you are going to clear varnish the hull, tapered planks definitely are the way to go. Refer to figure 4-4 as you read the following description.

First, measure the outside length of the largest frame. This is usually in the midships area of the hull. A piece of string wrapped around the outside of the frame will establish this dimension in inches. Divide this number by the width of a single plank. A typical plank width at midships is 3/8 inch. The number you calculate represents the number of planks required to cover the hull at that midships frame assuming a 3/8-inch plank width.

At the bow and stern, the planks need to be tapered to accommodate the same number of planks as at the midships frame due to their smaller frame sizes. Measure the bow and transom frame outside dimensions with string, and divide these numbers by the number of midships planks. This number tells you what the width of each plank at the transom and stem needs to be. With these three dimensions, you can uniformly taper the planks prior to putting them on the hull.

Some builders set up a router jig to taper each plank. This ensures uniform plank-to-plank fit. Since we are not talking about that many planks—perhaps 20 to 30—you could also simply mark and taper each plank by cutting and sanding. It is definitely worth all the work when it's done.

You can start tapered-width planking at either the sheers or the keelson. If you measured correctly, each plank should fall right in place with no further trimming required.

Constant-width plank hull. Since I always paint my own hulls, I use the faster constant-width plank method. using 5/16-inch to 3/8-inch-wide planks. Planking starts at the sheers and progresses toward the keelson. When I reach a point where it gets difficult to bend the planks into place, I switch to the keelson and work my way back toward the sheers. The last several planks have to be tapered at both ends to fit. You can see this in figure 4-3, my partially planked Phil Rhodes ketch Dogstar. It has 1/8-inch by 3/8-inch hard balsa planking over 1/4-inch poplar ply frames. It will be

Fig. 4-3I. Adding the cabin. The roof serves as a removable hatch. The cabin sides are 1/16-inch mahogany.

Fig. 4-3J. The removable cabin roof. Clear plastic wrap prevents glue from adhering to the cabin sides while the removable roof is built in place to ensure a tight fit.

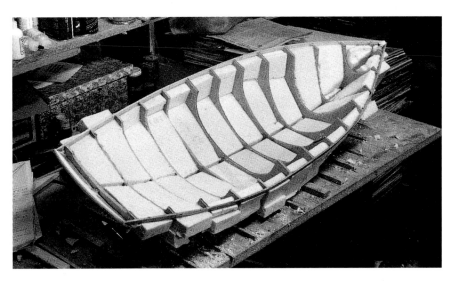

Fig. 4-3K. If you don't enjoy planking, here's an alternative: Use blue or pink insulating foam, glue the foam between adjacent frames, smooth the foam, and apply fiberglass and epoxy resin. DO NOT use polyester resin—it will attack the foam.

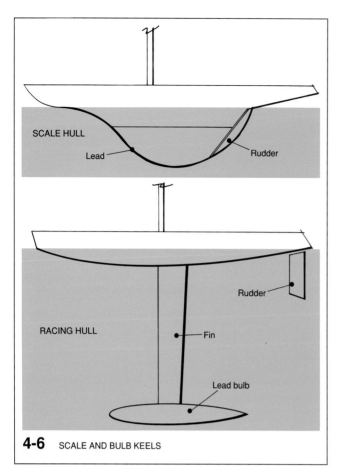

4-6 SCALE AND BULB KEELS

SCALE HULL

Lead

Rudder

RACING HULL

Rudder

Fin

Lead bulb

covered with one layer of 6-ounce fiberglass cloth and thinned epoxy resin. The hull is 39 inches long.

NOTE: When planking, always attach the planks in a symmetrical fashion. That is, do the first plank on the port (left) side, then add its counterpart in the same location on the starboard side. Never plank up one side of the hull and then the other. The planks must be alternated to equalize the bending stresses. Otherwise, you could end up with a misaligned hull.

Fiberglassing the hull. You have a couple of choices. You can use polyester resin, which is lighter than epoxy resin but has a horrendous odor. I believe this resin is toxic in an unventilated area so, if you use it, work outdoors or in a very well-ventilated area.

The second choice, and my favorite, is epoxy resin. It has much less odor and can be thinned with epoxy thinner, denatured alcohol, or acetone to a watery consistency. It is brushed easily onto the fiberglass cloth. However, I do know of several people who have developed allergic reactions to this resin, so be sure in both cases that your work area is well ventilated.

If you have never fiberglassed before, rest assured. It's as easy as brushing on a coat of paint. The trick is to use the correct weight fiberglass cloth and thinned polyester or epoxy

resin. Never apply unthinned resin. You end up with a lumpy mess that is almost impossible to sand off.

I use cheap 1-inch-wide brushes for this job and dispose of them when I'm finished. Epoxy resins are available from the hobby shops in 5-, 15-, and 30-minute varieties. The time refers to their pot life. I use the 30-minute variety. Epoxy and polyester resin thinners are available from just about all hardware retailers. The resin should be thinned to the consistency of water to make sure there's good brushout and complete wetting out of the fiberglass cloth.

Discarded glass bowls are good for mixing and thinning the resin. I usually mix 1 to 3 ounces at a time or just enough to completely cover the hull with one coat.

Before mixing the resin and thinner, cut the fiberglass cloth to size. Allow at least one inch of overlap at all points. If there are sharp bends or odd curves, such as at the stem, the cloth can be cut and overlapped as necessary. With the cloth cut and dry fitted, I brush on a coat of epoxy resin and then press the cloth in place, making sure that the cloth is snuggled down on the balsa planking.

The resin begins to soak into the cloth and wetting out becomes evident. The light areas indicate insufficient resin and possible air pockets. Brush more resin into those areas. If you cannot wet out an air pocket, prick it with a pin and press the cloth in place. The cloth should be completely saturated but not so much that the resin runs.

It's a good idea to gently squeegee off any excess resin. A small piece of Styrene or other plastic works well. This saves you a lot of sanding later.

After the first coat has cured, block sand the hull starting with 80 grit and ending at 220-grit paper. If the sandpaper tends to clog and fill with resin, the resin is probably not fully cured. Wait several hours and try again. A cool room really slows this process.

Try to sand off almost all of the resin above the cloth. Never sand

through the cloth. If you do, patch it with a small piece of cloth and resin and resand. Sanding into the fiberglass cloth itself will seriously weaken the skin strength. You know when you are cutting into the cloth when you begin to see white patches and the weave of the cloth. It should take no more than three coats of resin to completely fill the fiberglass cloth.

Keep in mind that epoxy and polyester resins are heavy. Too much resin is simply too much; a coat of resin much thicker than the cloth itself adds very little strength but a lot of weight. When the hull finally is sanded, spray on a light coat of auto body primer. This will show up all the high and low spots, not to mention the dings and dents that you didn't see before. Using auto body spot fillers, the sand-and-fill process starts all over again. This time, block sanding should start with 120 grit and progress to 400 grit. You probably will have to sand, fill, and prime two or three times to get a glassy-smooth hull.

Before you fiberglass the hull, here is a simple tip to get the bare hull ready to fiberglass. After the hull is planked, block sand across the planks rather than with the run of the planks. This quickly knocks off the plank edges and smoothly fairs the planks into each other. Fill low spots on the planking with one of the lightweight, spackle-type fillers. Don't use auto body fillers here. They are too hard and will not sand down with the balsa.

Another way to build a hull is to do fiberglass layups in a female mold. This process requires a male plug and female mold. But it allows you to hand lay up any number of identical fiberglass one-design hulls and be able to get as many as your club might need.

Figures 4-5A to 4-5G illustrate the steps to produce a male plug, female mold, and fiberglass hull for the International One-Design, a popular racing boat from the 1930s. Rolf Andersen built the mold as an Ozaukee Model Shipwrights Club project so that members could race a one-design scale class. Overall length is 48 inches. Hulls are laid up in this mold using one 12-ounce layer of cloth with two layers in the keel attach, transom, and stem areas.

If you decide to use this method, keep in mind that the fiberglass hulls are only as good as the male plug you start with. Rolf put in many hours sanding and filling the plank-on-frame plug before he fiberglassed it and then sanded and filled some more to get an absolutely glass-smooth hull. At the same time, of course, he made sure that the plug was straight and true.

When the plug was done, he con-

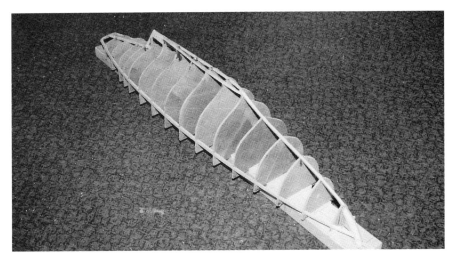

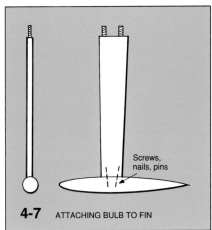

4-7 ATTACHING BULB TO FIN

Fig. 4-5A. This is the start of a 48-inch male plug over which a female mold will be formed. The shadows are an integral part of the male plug.

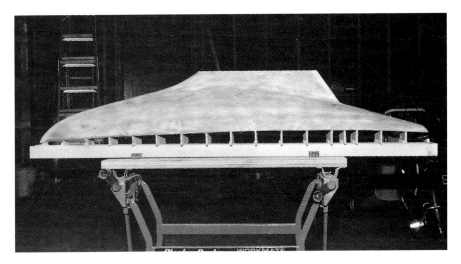

Fig. 4-5B. The male plug planked, fiberglassed and ready for primer and final filling and polishing. The lead keel will be added to the final product.

Fig. 4-5C. The male plug, off the building board. The plug has been primed, filled, painted, and polished to a mirror-smooth finish. There are two prime requisites for the male plug: it must be strong to withstand removal from the female mold, and it must have a glass-like finish. Every imperfection in the male plug will show up in the female mold and hulls made in this mold.

structed a large plywood box around it. The plug was rigidly mounted in the box with plenty of bracing. After coating the plug with a parting agent, Rolf covered it with several layers of fiberglass cloth and resin along with additional reinforcement. The object is to build a female mold that cannot flex in any way, so a dummy deck extending over the sheers was screwed to the male plug to define the mold parting lines.

After removing the plug from the mold, Rolf laid up several hulls using commercial thixotropic epoxy resin and gelcoat. Thixotropic is a fancy word that means the resin and gelcoat will not run when applied to a vertical surface—a handy feature when laying up hulls. The gelcoat is added first, and it becomes the color coat. With the gelcoat layer, color is molded in and painting is not necessary. The gelcoat is followed by a coat of epoxy resin and fiberglass cloth. Enough resin is used to completely saturate the cloth. And there is no exterior sanding required. Interior frames can be fiberglassed in as necessary to accommodate the keel, rudder post, transom, and radio board.

While this method is more expensive, it produces identical one-design hulls that are great for club events and beginners coming into the group. Both the labor and expense can be spread over a club membership.

For example, our club is in the process of developing a mold for our club racing class, the AMYA U. S. One Meter class. One of our members has volunteered to lay up the hulls, charging only for materials and labor. The club absorbs the mold and plug costs. This will allow new members with no previous boat building experience to get into racing easily at nominal expense.

Cold-molding. This is another way to build a strong and attractively finished hull. Using thin strips of hardwood veneer or cedar, you start by applying the first layer over a

Fig. 4-5D. The female mold box seen from the backside. Note the thick fiberglassing and plywood stiffeners to prevent the mold from flexing.

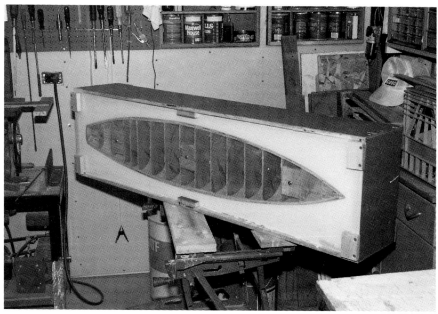

Fig. 4-5E. The female mold box seen from the lay-up or working side. The male plug is laying in the mold.

building form or strongback. The first layer is applied diagonally across the form. The individual strips are edge glued together and pinned or clamped to the form. The second layer is also applied diagonally but at right angles to the first layer. A third layer, if necessary, runs lengthwise stem to stern.

An average-sized 36-inch to 50-inch hull uses two or three layers of 1/32-inch by 3/8-inch strip wood. Just about any wood can be used to build up a beautiful clear-varnished hull. Due to their cold-molded ply construction, these hulls usually do not require any interior support other than deck beams and a king plank. Using this method, AMYA members have built hulls up to 6-feet long.

Vacuum-forming. Vacuum-forming plastic over a male plug is still another way to produce multiple copies of a one-design hull. However, this is not too practical for most builders due to the large vacuum table and pump required to form the plastic (not to mention the oven required to heat the plastic sheet).

Paper-mache. Although I have not tried paper-mache, I believe it would work. Once the various layers of newsprint or other paper are thoroughly dry, it is simple to varnish the hull inside and out. The rest of the hull is built in the usual way. The beauty of this method is that virtually any hull shape is feasible. Hulls could even be laid up inside a female mold, which is an interesting concept.

Foam insulation. One-inch-thick blue or pink foam insulation is another way to build a uniquely-shaped or difficult-to-plank hull. Using what was

called the "bread-and-butter method" from years ago, the foam is glued into as many layers as required to capture the hull outlines. The interior is hollowed out easily to accommodate the radio installation. Some thought must be given first to the keel and its attachment. Of itself, foam does not have the strength to support several pounds of lead. Fiberglass and plywood reinforcement would help.

Templates are used to ensure the hull shape is symmetrical and true to the original lines. One way to do this is to insert card or Styrene frame templates between the foam layers and to sand the foam down to these framelike stations. This method guarantees an accurately-shaped hull. After the foam is shaped it can be covered with lightweight fiberglass cloth (2 ounce) and epoxy resin. Do not use polyester resins on foam because they are not compatible. The resin dissolves the foam. Some of the foam can be left in to provide flotation. If you are building catamaran or trimaran hulls, you don't even need to remove the foam. Simply fiberglass right over the solid foam hull.

This method provides strong and light construction; and if you can find a construction site, the foam scraps provide you with enough material to build several hulls. Foam hulls need the usual reinforcing in the way of keel attach points, the rudder tube, the sheers, and the stem. If you assemble the card or plastic frames on a building board and then insert the foam blocks between the adjacent frames, the sheer strips can be added at the same time. This is easier than

doing it after the hull is done.

I used this method on one scale boat and it worked well. I definitely will use it again—perhaps next time on a racing hull. It's an excellent alternative if you don't like planking.

MAKING THE KEEL

The keel provides the necessary balance to keep the boat on its feet. Also, it opposes the tendency of the boat to move sideways or to make leeway when sailing to windward. Its shape provides hydrodynamic lift as the boat moves through the water. For this reason, the cross section of the keel is just as important as the shape of the sails.

A general rule of thumb for keel design is that keel depth is more effective than fore-to-aft keel width. If more keel is needed, it's better to go deeper than wider. This is true for two reasons: first, the deeper the weight, the longer the lever arm there is to offset the force of the sails; and second, a high-aspect-ratio keel, just like a glider wing, develops more hydrodynamic lift than a low-aspect-ratio shape.

Model boats use two basic keel styles. The fin-and-bulb type typically is used on non-scale AMYA racing classes. A lead bulb is attached to a thin high-aspect-ratio fin, which places the bulb well below the waterline. It provides great stability and plenty of hydrodynamic lift when going to windward.

The second style is the scale type. It follows the lines of whatever scale boat you happen to be building. This type is shaped to match the prototype keel outline. Some model designers deepen

Fig. 4-5F. The male plug removed from the female mold box. An actual laid-up hull is in the female mold. The 48-inch hull is made up of one layer of six-ounce cloth with reinforcements in the keel, bow, and rudder areas.

Fig. 4-5G. Here is the finished hull: an accurate model of the International One Design, a boat still being raced in Long Island and Bermuda.

the scale keel deliberately for the reasons mentioned above. They reason that when sailing, you can't see the keel anyway so it's not important, particularly when the stiffness and windward performances are improved.

Personally, all my scale boats get a scale keel. The deeper keels, in my opinion, are fine for all-out racing; but for puttering around the pond on a lazy Sunday afternoon, I prefer to maintain the scale outlines. Though the boat may be a bit more tender, I find it more challenging to sail. Keeps me on my toes.

Pictures of both keel types are shown in figure 4-6. Depending on the boat and the designer's recommendation, the lead bulb weighs typically from 4 to 10 pounds. The U. S. One Meter does very well on a 5-pound bulb, which, incidentally, by class rules can't be placed more than 14-1/4 inches below the bottom of the hull.

The amount of lead weight is not an arbitrary number. The hull needs to float on its designed waterline, and it also must balance fore and aft. When building an AMYA class racing hull, the designer always specifies the recommended bulb weight, size, and location of the bulb's center of gravity with respect to the fin.

Scale boats are not that simple.

Unless you are following someone else's construction plans, you are on your own when calculating the amount of lead you need.

The first thing to do is calculate the displacement. This process, while not too mathematically complicated, is beyond the scope of this book. The AMYA literature covers this in detail. Any yacht design book also explains this procedure.

Let's assume you or your marine architect brother-in-law have calculated the displacement of your Tahiti ketch to be 12 pounds That is, when floating on its lines, it displaces 12 pounds of water.

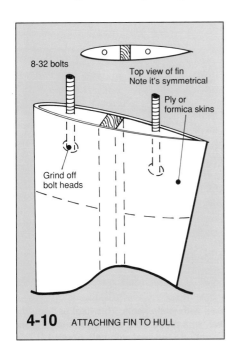

8-32 bolts

Top view of fin
Note it's symmetrical

Ply or
formica skins

Grind off
bolt heads

4-10 ATTACHING FIN TO HULL

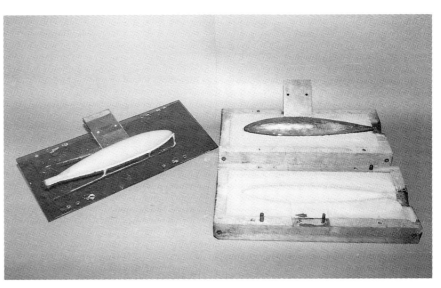

Fig. 4-8A. The original pattern for an AMYA U. S. One Meter class 5-pound lead bulb is on the left. A plate splits it lengthwise to allow the two plaster halves to be cast simultaneously. See the right side.

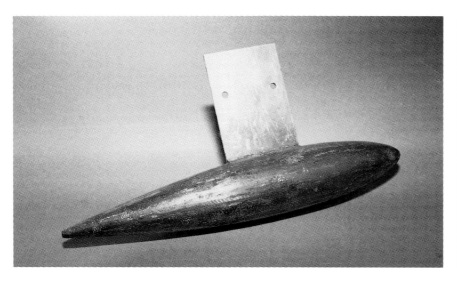

Fig. 4-8B. The finished lead bulb cleaned up and ready to attach to the keel fin. The extension is .090-inch aluminum.

Fig. 4-8C. The bulb mounted on an AMYA U. S. One Meter class boat.

You should allow approximately 3-1/2 pounds for the bare hull, deck installation, radio, spars, rigging, and sails, along with the sail winch. Subtracting this weight from the 12-pound calculated displacement leaves us with 8-1/2 pounds of keel weight. Because the displacement calculations include the keel, you can figure out where to establish the keel-to-hull parting line to get the lead weight you need.

Water has a very high coefficient of drag. A lot of energy is wasted just trying to move the boat through the water. To reduce drag, AMYA members have done a lot of experimentation with bulb profiles, including various NASA shapes. Data is available from the AMYA on these shapes.

When attaching the fin to the hull, it's very important not to have any angles coming together at less than 90 degrees. Use smooth fillets at the fin-to-hull junction, and round off the top of the rudder where it meets the hull.

These intersections are great drag-producing sites.

The fore and aft location of the bulb on the fin is very important: the bulb must be placed so that the center of gravity of the bulb is at the center of buoyancy of the hull. Also, if the bulb is placed too far forward on the fin, it can cause the fin to twist, which, in turn, causes the bulb and fin to vibrate. This creates additional drag and slows the boat. The trend in new AMYA designs is to put the leading edge of the bulb very close to the leading edge of the fin. This virtually eliminates bulb oscillation.

The problem is demonstrated easily when riding in a boat. If you put your hand in the water when the boat is underway, you'll feel the pressure and resistance change as you vary the angle of your hand. At some angle, your hand begins to vibrate or oscil-

late as it tries to find a neutral point. The same thing happens to the model boat fin when going to windward. And the lead bulb, because of its great mass in front of the fin, simply amplifies the problem. Fin construction must be absolutely rigid.

A typical bulb outline is shown in figure 4-6. The bulb is round in cross section and symmetrical in plan view. Winged keels are beginning to appear now on the bigger boats such as the AMYA g-Forse class. While the winged keel on a full-size boat provides a greater righting moment with less depth than a bulb keel, in my opinion their worth on anything smaller than 72-inch hulls is questionable.

The bulb is attached to the fin with screws or pins driven into the lead and anchored in the fin with epoxy. Alternate methods are to use an aluminum plate cast into the bulb and

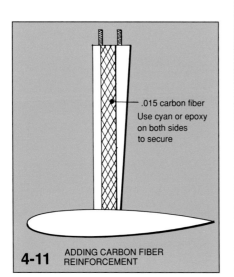

.015 carbon fiber
Use cyan or epoxy
on both sides
to secure

4-11 ADDING CARBON FIBER REINFORCEMENT

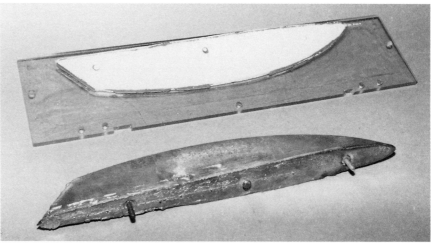

Fig. 4-9A. The same lead-casting process is used with scale keels. This keel pattern, the International One Design with finished lead keel, was made from dense foam and glued to acrylic sheet. The keel attach bolts are cast right into the keel when it's poured.

Fig. 4-9B. The two-part female plaster mold made from the foam pattern in figure 4-9A.

pin, or epoxy the plate into the fin. The fin-to-bulb joint can be reinforced and filleted with fiberglass cloth and resin (figure 4-7).

Typically, the bulb is cast in two halves in a plaster or wood mold and then epoxied together. Or it can be cast in one piece in a two-piece mold. The mold is separated after the lead has cooled. (See figures 4-8A to 4-8C.)

Scale boat keels can be made by pouring molten lead into a one- or two-piece mold (figures 4-9A and 4-9B), or they can be loose-lead-shot secured in the hull with epoxy resin. In the latter method, lead shot is poured into the hull and hollow keel interior. The empty hull is floated in a tub of water, and enough lead shot is poured in and

distributed fore and aft to float the hull on her lines. Be sure to allow the requisite extra 3 to 3-1/2 pounds for the deck, mast, sail winch, batteries, and radio installation. (I always include this weight when I pour the lead shot.) Epoxy resin is poured in to secure the lead afterward.

The advantage of this method is that you do not have to melt lead, which is a somewhat hazardous pastime at best. One disadvantage is that for a given volume, the keel is not quite as heavy as solid lead. Another advantage is that you do not have to calculate the displacement. You simply pour in enough lead plus the extra 3 pounds to float the hull at the waterline. On a scale design, chances are the lead shot won't be above the top of the hollow keel.

If you're building an AMYA racing class boat, the chances are good that you can buy a precast bulb in the weight you need. Most common weights are readily available.

If you elect to pour your own keel in a plaster mold, make sure the plaster is fully cured and there is no moisture anywhere in or near the mold. Molten lead hitting any moisture turns it to

steam instantly, possibly with catastrophic results, so please be careful.

Cast 8-32 keel bolts right into scale keels that are going to be through-bolted to the hull. It's a good idea to add a thin layer of silicone rubber tub caulk to the keel-to-hull juncture. Rubber faucet washers inside also help seal the hull and keep that pesky water out of the bilges.

There are several ways to construct a high-aspect-ratio fin for an AMYA type racing hull. You can use 1/32-inch to 1/16-inch ply as the outer skins, which are joined with a spacer in between to form a symmetrically-shaped cross section. At the top of the fin bolts or a tongue attach to the hull. The fin must be super stiff, and there must not be any torsional twisting or lateral flexing of the fin. It must be stiff enough to support the lead bulb when the boat is laid over at a 50-degree angle in heavy air, and it cannot vibrate or oscillate when going to windward.

Formica has been used successfully in thicknesses from 1/32 inch to 1/16 inch. On the U. S. One Meter class, 1/16-inch ply faired with 1/8-inch balsa on both sides has worked well for me. I add a .015-inch thick by 1/2-inch-wide layer of carbon fiber to the fin on both sides to really stiffen the fin. (figure 4-11.) You can use epoxy or CYA glue to attach the carbon fiber.

The fin is through-bolted to the hull using 8-32 bolts or bigger, depending on the size of the hull (figure 4-10). The keelson area inside the boat is reinforced where the bolts come through the hull. This is a high-stress area, so it's a good idea to get into the habit of picking up your boat by the fin or keel rather than the hull itself. The designer provides instructions on how to reinforce the hull and on fin construction and through-bolt sizes.

An alternate way to attach the fin to the hull is the tongue-and-box method. There is a projecting plywood tongue on the fin that slides into a box built into the hull. This method

Fig. 4-12. A U.S. One Meter boat with typical deck beam installation. This builder elected to make a non-rectangular hatch opening. The opening should be large enough so everything inside is accessible and removable.

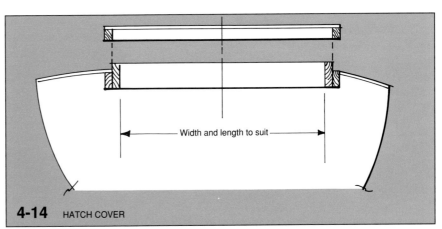

Width and length to suit

4-14   HATCH COVER

Fig. 4-13. Here's a simple way to come up with a planked deck. Use 1/8-inch balsa as a sub-deck, over which 1/32-inch by 1/4- or 3/8-inch wide mahogany veneer strips are glued. Either yellow or white glue will work well. Both cure slowly, giving you time to position the planks and basswood strips. Highlight planking by alternating the planks with 1/32-inch square basswood strips. Then sand and varnish. First block sand lightly with 120, then 220-grit sandpaper until the deck surface is smooth. I varnish a deck like this with several coats of polyurethane. Thinned epoxy will also do the job. It's a simple process and looks great.

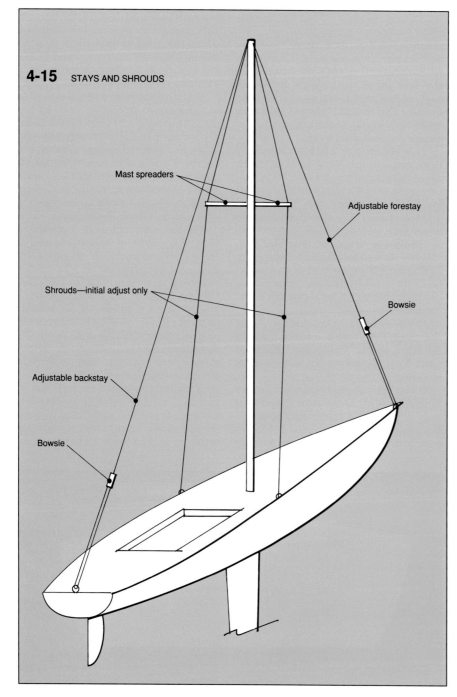

increases hull strength considerably because the box runs from the keelson up to the deck king plank. Also it reduces the chance of water getting into the hull. I have used both the bolt and tongue-and-box methods, and they seem to work fine. The bolt method might be a little less work to install. It's probably best, at least initially, to follow the designer's specifications.

DECKS AND ACCESS HATCHES

Weight-conscious racing skippers consider the fabric deck to be the ultimate solution. Various heat-shrink, self-adhesive, plastic films intended to cover RC aircraft are attached to the sheer strips of the hull and then heat shrunk to a drum-tight finish. An iron is used to activate the covering's adhesive. The deck must be specially prepared to use this method, so I do not recommend it for beginning boat builders. If the edges are not sealed well, the deck edges can lift; and if you don't see it before you launch you could end up with a very soggy boat interior.

For the new builder/skipper, either 1/64-inch or 1/32-inch plywood works quite well. The plywood is rough cut to size and glued in place with epoxy. Plenty of masking tape holds the deck in place while the epoxy is curing. Just be sure to seal the inside of the ply before it's attached to the hull. I learned the hard way that you can't varnish those interior portions of the deck where they contact the king plank and cross members. After several trips to the pond, one of my decks separated from the hull in several places. Fortunately, I caught it between sailing sessions.

Figure 4-12 shows a U. S. One Meter hull ready for deck installation. Note the king plank running down the center of the hull, the arced cross members, and the framed-in hatch opening.

Some builders construct their decks using 1/16-inch to 1/8-inch balsa sheet covered with 3/4-ounce fiberglass. This

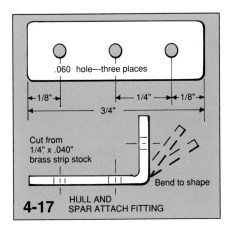

.060 hole—three places

1/8" | 1/4" | 1/8"

3/4"

Cut from
1/4" x .040"
brass strip stock

Bend to shape

4-17 HULL AND
SPAR ATTACH FITTING

method works well with highly crowned decks.

For the scale boat where you want to go the extra mile, a hardwood-planked deck is in order. Strips approximately 3/8-inch wide and perhaps 1/32-inch to 1/16-inch thick are attached to a balsa or ply sub-deck that is varnished or otherwise sealed on its interior surface. Black construction paper between adjacent planks simulates caulked seams. After the glues sets, the paper is sanded flush with the deck.

Figure 4-13 shows another way to simulate caulked deck planks, using alternating 1/32-inch by 3/8-inch mahogany strips and 1/32-inch-square basswood strips. I did this over a balsa sub-deck by coating the balsa with a thin glue layer and alternating the dark mahogany and light basswood strips. I pencilled in reference lines on the balsa to keep the planks parallel to the deck centerline. This is an easy task that looks quite complicated when it's finished.

In fact, this method of alternating light and dark veneers creates all kinds of inlaid deck and hull patterns

on any type of sailboat. It adds little weight but can sure dress up an otherwise drab boat. This process can be used as the last layer of a cold-molded hull. Alternating wood colors surely produces a knock-out boat.

You need access hatches in the deck to allow you to get at and maintain the equipment inside. Unfortunately, any openings you cut into the hull are potential water entry points. Hatches must be watertight but you cannot add so much protection that you incur a weight penalty.

Hatches must be sealed with tight-fitting hatch covers. Water has a way of getting into the hull through the tiniest openings on a windy day when the boat is being sailed hard. Figure 4-14 shows one way to build a simple, reliable, and watertight hatch cover.

This is the method I use on all my racing boats. After I install the deck I install the framing that extends above it. Then I cover this framed opening with clear plastic kitchen wrap. I build the removable hatch cover frame and cover in place right over the deck framing. This method ensures a very tight fit that can be made even more secure by a rubber band across the top of the hatch as a hold down.

It's also a good idea to attach the hatch cover to the hull with a light-weight line. Hatch covers came off twice for me while sailing, so it can happen to you! One actually floated back to shore, the other went to Davey Jones' locker.

Usually, I add a second flush-mounted hatch cover right above the rudder tube. Then, if the rudder horn loosens (which it has), I can get at the errant setscrew to retighten it. This hatch, due to its infrequent opening, is held in place with two No. 2 wood-screws and the hatch cover is set flush

with the deck. Unless you can get your hand back there from the main hatch and be able to hold and turn an Allen wrench, I highly recommend that you add a rudder hatch.

A good rule of thumb for your hatch openings is to make them as small as possible. All openings weaken the deck's strength and are potential leaks. Ease and reliability are also important. Although rubber bands are not very pleasing to look at, they do work well and they don't add weight. Some skippers use various vinyl tapes and seal the hatch after every closure. Fancy internal locking methods add weight and can fail while screws are clumsy and can fall into the grass at the pond. Keep it simple.

SPARS AND RIGGING

Spars are the lumber used to hold the sails aloft. They are the mast, main sail boom, and the jib sail boom (more commonly called the jib club). These spars in racing boats are as light as the serious skipper can make or buy them.

To be competitive, a racing boat has all weight above the waterline absolutely minimized. The trend among the various racing classes has been to low-mass, high-strength materials such as carbon fiber. Some skippers also use balsa or spruce covered with carbon fiber. Others use solid carbon fiber masts and booms which are

Fig. 4-16. You can make simple shroud and stay attach points from 1/4-inch brass strip attached to the deck with brass screws. Radio control aircraft steel clevises attach to these brackets. Do not use nylon clevises; they can twist off the brackets. The 2-56 threaded rod that screws into the clevis is easily bent back on itself, wrapped with copper wire, and soldered to form a closed eye.

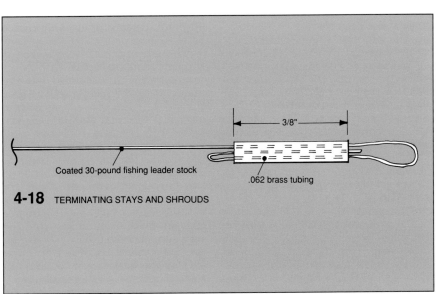

3/8"

Coated 30-pound fishing leader stock

.062 brass tubing

4-18 TERMINATING STAYS AND SHROUDS

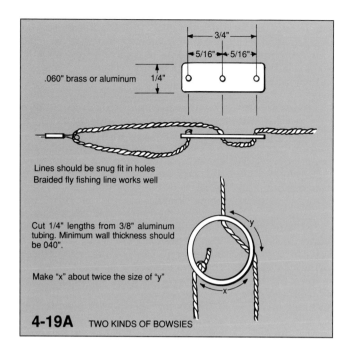

Lines should be snug fit in holes
Braided fly fishing line works well

Cut 1/4" lengths from 3/8" aluminum tubing. Minimum wall thickness should be 040".

Make "x" about twice the size of "y"

4-19A TWO KINDS OF BOWSIES

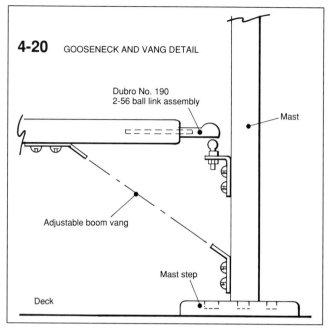

4-20 GOOSENECK AND VANG DETAIL

Dubro No. 190
2-56 ball link assembly

Mast

Adjustable boom vang

Mast step

Deck

very expensive. It's all in how much you want to spend. These lightweight materials help the boat's performance, but if your sailing skills have not caught up with your boat, don't bother. Sail first, buy high-tech gear later.

My recommendation for beginners is a method I have used on both racing and scale boats: find a piece of clear spruce (Sitka if you can find it) or pine, and rip your spars from it. The operative word here is "clear." Don't use something that's full of knots because they create fracture areas.

Pop-Up Manufacturing has reasonably priced extruded aluminum masts in both 72-inch and 85-inch lengths, and several members of our club have used them for several racing seasons. They are an excellent compromise between weight aloft and structural stiffness. They require very little bracing, whereas the wood masts require substantial rigging and adjusting to keep them dead straight.

A logical choice of spar material for your first racing boat is aluminum. In my opinion, for that scale boat there is only one choice: pine or spruce finished with several coats of spar varnish. The bright finish sets off the finished boat and gives it a salty look.

Now, we need something to hold up that towering mast. As shown in figure 4-15, the lines that run from either side of the mast-head to the deck are called shrouds. The lines that run to the bow and stern are called stays. Hence, we have a backstay (stern) and a forestay (bow). The shrouds are adjustable only to permit vertical placement of the mast. The shrouds and stays are terminated at the deck with fittings that allow easy removal of the mast for transportation

and storage.

Incidentally, while I have shown a forestay in figure 4-15, it is not usually used on racing boats. The jibstay and jib swivel take care of this function. If a forestay is used, it is used as insurance against the jib swivel or jibstay parting. Underway, the forestay is kept loose so it doesn't interfere with the backstay and jibstay tension. I always put one on my scale boats because it was part of the prototype, and it adds to the complexity of the rigging. For more information on the function of the backstay and jibstay, see Chapter 6.

Figure 4-16 shows how RC aircraft steel clevises can be used to terminate shrouds and stays. If you use these clevises, do not use the nylon style (they can twist loose); and be sure to use the plastic keepers that come with them. With the twisting action imposed on them, they can come undone in a good blow.

The 2-56 size is fine for boats up to 65 inches long. A piece of 2-56 threaded rod is required for each clevis. I screw the rod into the clevis and then bend the rod into a closed loop. The loop is wrapped with soft copper wire and soldered so that the stay or shroud connected to this loop cannot slip out. This is a simple and inexpensive fastener that will not fail and that is easily disconnected when necessary. I have not experienced a failure in several years of sailing.

I terminate the shrouds and stays at the deck, mast, and booms with fittings cut from .062-inch by 1/4-inch brass strip. This stock is available at hobby shops and hardware stores. Look for the K & S Engineering brass point-of-purchase display. The fittings

are attached to the hull and spars with No. 2 x 3/8-inch brass wood-screws. See figure 4-17 for a sketch.

You can gang-produce enough fittings for a boat in an hour or less. Lay out the 1/4-inch hole spacings on the brass strip, drill all the holes with a 1/16-inch diameter drill bit, and cut the pieces at 3/4-inch intervals. I have used this type of fitting since I started sailing; I can assure you they work regardless of boat size. Always use two woodscrews to attach each fitting.

I have seen a number of different shroud and stay materials used: stainless monofilament, stranded steel wire, various woven synthetics, and fishing line of all types. My personal preference is stranded steel fishing leader coated with black or clear plastic. Available at well-stocked fishing supply stores in 30-foot lengths, it is available in several strengths from 15-pound to 45-pound. Usually I buy the 30-pound rating. It doesn't rust or break.

The shrouds and stays are run through their respective fittings and terminated with a crimped 1/16-inch diameter by 3/8-inch length of brass tubing. I crimp the tubing with an electrical terminal staking tool. (See figure 4-18.) On a particularly windy day a few years ago, I lost the whole sail rig over the side because one of my shroud crimps let go. Since then, I put two shrouds on each side of the boat. It doesn't add weight and almost does nothing for windage, but it sure does give me piece of mind knowing that each shroud crimp is only carrying half the load it was before. This is not necessary on the backstay or forestay; the shrouds carry the greatest loads.

The backstay, jibstay, and forestay (if

you use one) must be adjustable to permit raking of the mast fore and aft. This allows the skipper to precisely tune the boat for that day's weather picture. (See Chapter 6 for more information on tuning.)

Bowsies provide quick and simple line adjustment. They have no moving parts and can be made from plastic, aluminum, or brass. I have had poor luck with plastic; it tends to crack and fail at the wrong time. Aluminum is easy to fabricate and will not break. I cut mine from 1/16-inch by 1/4-inch stock. See figures 4-19A and 4-19B for the proper threading arrangement and general dimensions.

Bowsies work with just about any kind of line, but the hole diameter and bowsie material must be matched to the thickness and finish of the line. Bowsies rely on the friction of the line running through the bowsie. If the hole is too large or the line is too smooth, the line slips and causes problems when underway. It's a good idea to test hole size versus line materials while you are still in the shop. The last thing you want or need is a self-adjusting backstay when you are running for the finish line. (See figure 4-15 for bowsie locations.)

Fishing snaps are handy to terminate the stays and sheets at the booms, but avoid the smaller sizes. They are not strong enough in a good blow. The forces at work on the sails, mast, and rigging in a 15-miles-per-hour wind are much greater than you might think.

There are a number of ways to connect the main boom to the mast. Figure 4-20 shows a simple method using hobby shop components. I use the 2-56 size ball link assemblies for boats up to 600 square inches. Above that, I use the 4-40 size, which is much more heavy duty. The threaded rod is screwed into the nylon ball, and the other end (approximately 2 inches) is glued into a 1/16-inch hole drilled in the end of the boom. There is also commercial hardware available for those who do not want to do it themselves.

The boom vang keeps the main sail boom from twisting upward as the sail swings out. It is absolutely necessary to keep the boom at right angles to the mast at all times. When going to windward with the sails sheeted tightly in, this is not a problem. However, when sailing off the wind with the boom swung out, the wind tries to lift the sail, which in effect dumps the air and reduces sail drive. The vang prevents this from happening. On smaller boats, a bowsie and fishing line will suffice; larger boats require something more substantial like a brass turnbuckle and steel fishing leader. It should be made adjustable (figure 4-22).

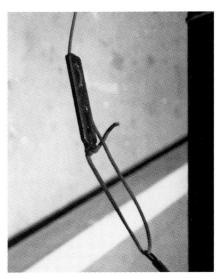

Fig. 4-19B. Two Bowsie methods. I prefer the flat plates (right) because they're easier to make, but both work well. The donut type may slip less than the flat plate type.

Fig. 4-21. A scratchbuilt gooseneck and boom vang. The extruded aluminum mast stock is available from Pop-Up Mfg. The mast can be moved fore and aft for sail trim. Use fairleads at the sheet exits in the hull to reduce line friction and consequent wear.

Fig. 4-22. You can cut mast spreaders from aluminum sheet; 1/16-inch thickness is best. An alternate method is brass tubing flattened and drilled at the ends where the shrouds pass through.

5

RADIO INSTALLATION AND CONTROL

THE RADIO system breathes life into a sailboat. Without it, there is no control; the sailboat is a free spirit. With it, the boat becomes an extension of your mind, doing exactly what you tell it to do. A radio enables you, the onshore skipper, to sail the boat as if you were on board with your hand on the tiller.

It puts you at the helm, handling the jib and main sheets, controlling the rudder, and trimming the sails in order to wring the last little bit of speed out of the boat. And if you think you'd like to race, the radio allows you to use the same strategy and tactics as Dennis Connor may have used aboard Stars and Stripes. Hitting the line right at the gun, tacking duels, stealing the other guy's wind, and finding better air is all part of the fun at your fingertips. Crossing the line on a port tack right at the gun and beating to that first mark with a bunch of other boats right behind you will really curl your toes!

Today's radios are so reliable that system reliability is essentially dependent on the amount of attention the skipper gives to his radio and how it's installed in the boat. The radio itself is unlikely to fail, but skipper-caused problems can and do occur: inadequately-charged batteries, bilge water in the receiver or servos, loose and sloppily mounted components, overloaded sail winches, defective connectors, and the like. These kinds of problems raise havoc with the best of skippers, and they always seem to happen in the middle of a crucial race. (Murphy's Law prevents these things from ever happening on shore.) Radio care and feeding are very important to consistent reliability at the pond.

The radio you buy comes with charging and maintenance instructions. To stay out of trouble, follow these instructions to the letter!

RUDDER AND SAIL CONTROL

To fully control the boat at all times, plan on using both rudder and sail control. If you are not going to race and simply want to putter around the pond, you may, depending on the boat, be able to get by without a sail winch. However, the lack of sail control severely limits your boat's performance as compared to one with sail control. If you plan to race and really want to make the boat go where you want it to, you'll need sail control.

Serious racing skippers like to add other functions such as jib twitchers,

Fig. 5-1A. A typical two-channel radio installation. The hand-held transmitter is in the back. In the front from left to right: sail winch, receiver, battery pack and rudder servo.

Fig. 5-1B. The onboard radio receiver. The rudder servo plugs into the "rudder" connection. The sail winch plugs into the "throttle" connection. The antenna can be run up the backstay or the mast, or it can be strung out in the hull interior.

Fig. 5-1C. Typical rudder servo. The ouput arm swings approximately 45 degrees to either side of the neutral point.

downhaul adjusters, and backstay tensioners. However, until you have mastered the art of steering the shortest route between two points with the best sail trim, forget about the go-fast options. It's confusing enough learning to steer the boat, setting the sails for best speed, and keeping one eye on the other skippers without also having to decide when to tighten the backstay, set the jib twitcher, or adjust the downhaul—particularly when the wind is blowing 20 miles per hour!

THE TWO-CHANNEL RADIO

The most commonly used sailboat radio is the inexpensive, two-channel configuration. Airtronic, Aristo-craft, and Futaba manufacture extremely reliable, low-cost models. If you already have a four-channel radio, go ahead and use it. Just disregard the extra channels. As your skills grow you can use the other channels.

Figures 5-1A and 5-1C show the components that make up a typical two-channel radio: hand-held transmitter, receiver and battery pack, and rudder servo. Two-channnel radios come with two servos, but only one is used. A more powerful sail servo, or winch, as it's more commonly called, is substituted for the second servo.

FREQUENCY CONTROL

The Federal Communications Commission (FCC) regulates all model radio channel assignments and transmissions. They have divided the available channels into two groups: aircraft and surface. (Surface covers boats and cars.) By FCC regulation, it is illegal to use an aircraft radio to control a surface model, or a surface radio to control an aircraft. All surface channels are in the 75-megahertz band, and all aircraft channels are in the 72-megahertz band.

There is one notable exception: the 27-megahertz citizens band, which can be used for both aircraft and surface use. There are six of these channels (channels A1 to A6); usually they're used with surface models. Rarely are they used with aircraft because of potential interference problems.

Currently there are 15 surface channels available for use in the 75-megahertz band; these are even-numbered channels from 62 through 90. Odd-numbered channels will soon be available. Therefore, the sailing skipper has more than enough channels available to stage regattas.

Before you buy your radio, check with your local club (if there is one in the area) to see what channels are open. Is there anyone at your pond solo sailing? If so, what channel are they on? Avoid same-channel conflicts. You won't be able to sail until the

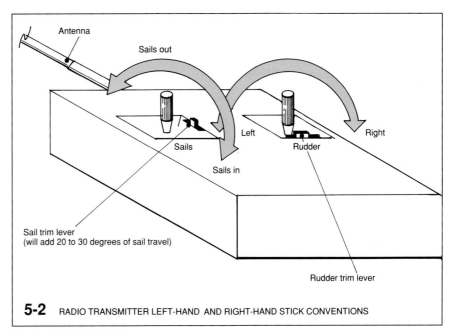

5-2 RADIO TRANSMITTER LEFT-HAND AND RIGHT-HAND STICK CONVENTIONS

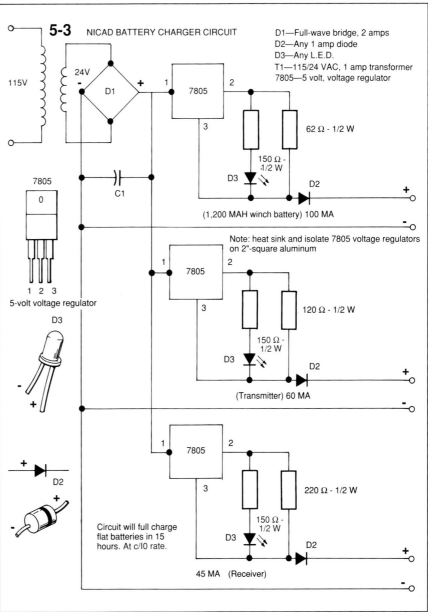

5-3 NICAD BATTERY CHARGER CIRCUIT

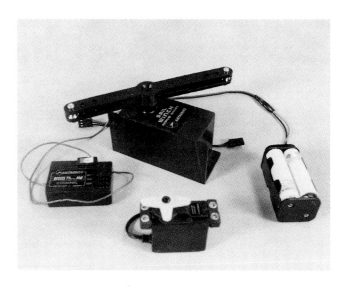

Fig. 5-4. An Airtronic sail winch, receiver, rudder servo, and 4.8-volt nicad battery pack.

Fig. 5-5. A Futaba S-25 sail winch with Airtronic radio.

other skipper turns off his transmitter.

Remember, too, that you should not turn on your transmitter until you are sure you are the only one at the pond on that channel. It could be very dangerous if someone was driving a fast gas-powered boat and lost control of it because you inadvertently turned on your transmitter and it was on his channel. In the middle of a sailboat race, you would have one very unhappy skipper on your hands, particularly if he was out in front when "you shot him down." Besides, it's only courteous.

Most clubs maintain a list of channels being used by each member so that channel conflicts are minimized.

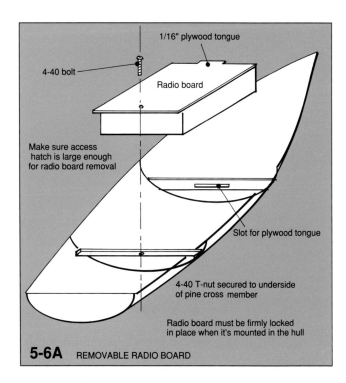

1/16" plywood tongue

4-40 bolt

Radio board

Make sure access hatch is large enough for radio board removal

Slot for plywood tongue

4-40 T-nut secured to underside of pine cross member

Radio board must be firmly locked in place when it's mounted in the hull

5-6A REMOVABLE RADIO BOARD

It should be updated regularly for the members.

With so many channels available, it shouldn't be difficult to find an open channel. But if you can't, there are radios available that allow you to change channels right at the pond by simply plugging a different set of crystals into the transmitter and receiver. At regional and national regattas, it may be mandatory for each skipper to have up to 3 channels available per boat.

SAIL TRIM AND STEERING

As shown in figure 5-2, it is standard practice to use the left-hand transmitter stick for sail control and the right-hand stick for rudder control. The left stick can only be moved vertically by the skipper. As you move the stick up, the sail winch will ease the sails out. As you move the stick down, the winch hauls the sails in. The sails can be set to all positions, from closehauled (sailing to windward) to all the way out (running before the wind).

The right stick controls the rudder in the same way, but it is limited to horizontal motion. The further the stick is moved right or left, the more corresponding rudder

travel is fed in. When the stick is neutralized, the rudder centers. The rudder servo on the boat is fast enough to virtually duplicate stick movements in real time.

Located next to each stick are small trim levers. They allow the skipper to add or perhaps subtract small amounts of rudder and sail trim much like a pilot would use aileron trim to pick up a heavy wing. This eliminates having to hold in small trim corrections at the sticks.

BATTERIES

Most two-channel radios are sold without batteries. They are designed to be used with AA-size alkaline dry cells or rechargeable nicads. While a fresh set of alkaline dry cells lasts for two or three months of weekly sailing, most skippers seem to prefer the rechargeable nicads and a purchased or homemade charger. You can start with dry cells and convert to nicads later.

The transmitter battery consists of 8 AA-size cells in series totalling 9.6 volts. The receiver uses 4 AA-size cells totalling 4.8 volts. Both batteries are usually rated at 500 to 600 milliampere hour (mah) capacity. However, you can use higher capacity batteries in the boat (up to 1,200 mah) to handle high winds and large sail areas, or simply to extend the battery life between charges.

Batteries and chargers can be purchased from the radio manufacturer or you can purchase the nicads locally and build or buy a charger. I found several good 50-mah chargers at the local scientific surplus outlet that originally were intended for use as small calculator battery eliminators. The plug-in jacks even fit my transmitter. But if they do not match, chances are Radio Shack has a jack that will fit your transmitter. For the receiver, you

Fig. 5-6B. Radio board installation in a fiberglass scale boat hull. Note the two wing nuts holding the aft end of the radio board to the hull. The rudder pushrod and winch output arm must be disconnected when the radio board is removed from the hull.

Fig. 5-6C. Another radio board installation. This one is retained with two screws and a tongue. Note the rudder cables. The winch is controlling three sails—hence the three sheets.

can buy a matching male and female set.

Two chargers are required: one for the transmitter and one for the receiver. Make sure that the charger rating matches the mah capacity of your battery packs. The C10 charging rule mandates the charge rate of a depleted nicad battery pack should be 1/10 of the milliampere-hour rating of the battery for 14 hours to 16 hours. For example: a 500-mah battery should not be charged at a rate higher than 50 milliamperes, a 1,200-mah battery should not be charged at a rate higher than 120 milliamperes.

There are a number of simple charger circuits that easily can be built at home. Figure 5-3 shows a circuit that I have used for several years with batteries ranging from 500 mah to 1,200 mah. The LED indicator lights when charging current is flowing to the battery. If the indicator is

not lit, the charging circuit is open and the battery is not being charged. All components for this charger are readily available from your local Radio Shack store.

You can package the charger in any type of insulated box, but make sure that the circuit is adequately enclosed so there is no danger of electrical shock. A few holes in the case are sufficient for ventilation. The plastic handy-boxes with aluminum covers sold at Radio Shack work well and provide a place for the on/off switch, LED indicators and fuse holder.

SAIL WINCHES

There is a broad selection of sail winches available. Your choice will be dictated by the sail area of your boat, the speed at which you want the winch to operate, the amount of weight you can afford to devote to the winch, and finally, how much you are willing to spend.

Winch installation is really a topic in itself and is covered in detail in Chapter 7. However, some consideration needs to be given here as relates to the onboard battery and radio installation.

The Airtronic winch shown in Figure 5-4 will handle sail areas up to around 900 square inches. Having a very high gear reduction ratio, it is not a very fast winch, but it is extremely powerful. It is an excellent all-around winch for use in both racing and scale boats where high torque is required to haul in the sails, and it is plug-compatible with Airtronic receivers.

Since the winch usually draws its power directly from the receiver battery, consideration needs to be given to the receiver battery's ability to meet the amperage requirements of the winch. This requirement has to be sustained for at least a couple of hours of sailing. As wind speeds increase, the

Fig. 5-7A. This shows the radio board being fitted into a 39-inch hull. Only the rudder servo has been installed on the radio board. This rudder uses cables rather than a solid pushrod.

Fig. 5-7B. The complete radio board for a U.S. One Meter boat. The sail winch is a Futaba S-25. The radio board is built of light weight poplar plywood and heavily varnished. Note the on/off slide switch.

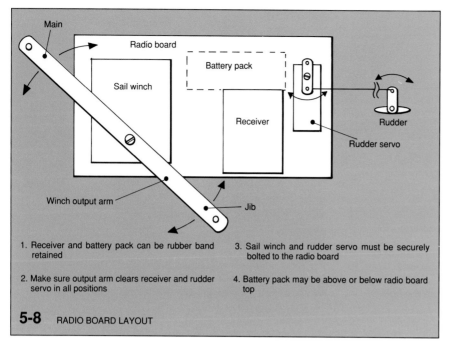

Main
Radio board
Battery pack
Sail winch
Receiver
Rudder
Winch output arm
Rudder servo
Jib

1. Receiver and battery pack can be rubber band retained

2. Make sure output arm clears receiver and rudder servo in all positions

3. Sail winch and rudder servo must be securely bolted to the radio board

4. Battery pack may be above or below radio board top

5-8 RADIO BOARD LAYOUT

load on the sail winch also increases. This in turn puts a heavier drain on the receiver battery. The sail winch can deplete a 500-mah receiver battery in an hour or less if the sail loads are great enough to periodically stall the winch.

For boats under 40 inches and carrying 600 square inches of sail or less, the compact Futaba S-25 winch shown in figure 5-5 is a good choice. It is plug-compatible with Futaba two-channel radios and comes with a ready-to-use winch arm. It is smaller and lighter than the Airtronic winch but does not deliver as much torque.

In a U. S. One Meter boat with winds gusting to 25 miles per hour, this winch could deplete a fully charged 500-mah pack in one hour of continuous sailing. So, it's a good idea to carry an extra fully charged receiver battery for those unexpected windy days.

THE RADIO BOARD— MOUNTING AND REMOVING

Your radio and batteries should be fastened securely to a radio board, which is mounted in the hull and also contains the rudder servo and sail winch. Some skippers also mount the receiver on/off switch here. The radio board must be removable, lightweight, and impervious to any water that gets into the hull, regardless of how much the boat is heeled. No matter how tight you batten the access hatch, you will take on water on a windy day with the deck awash. Not much maybe, but you will take on water.

A typical, functional board layout is shown in figure 5-8. Note that there are as many ways to lay out the board

as there are skippers. The important thing is to make sure the rudder pushrod and sail winch arm do not get fouled as they move. And the rudder pushrod must have a straight and clear route to the rudder post.

The bottom line for radio boards is to keep everything as simple as possible. Complicated components may look nice, but they can fail at the wrong time. Spending a Sunday at the pond should be a pleasant experience, and keeping it simple goes a long way toward that objective.

It's a good idea to mount the radio board so there is at least 1/2 inch of clearance between any of the radio board components and the interior skin of the hull. I did not always do this; then one day my rudder servo failed because it was waterlogged. Later, I poured a tablespoon of water out of that servo. The servo had barely cleared the bottom of the hull and as water came into the bilges, it wicked right into the servo.

No two radio boards are alike, but there are a few universal layout considerations. The rudder servo should be mounted at the aft end of the board to allow the rudder pushrod to run straight aft to the rudder post. The sail winch control arm must be free to swing through a 180-degree arc without snagging the main and jib sheet lines or striking the interior of the hull. The board must be securely fastened to the hull and be easily removable for maintenance, component replacement, and hull inspection and repair.

Weight is another important consideration. Racing skippers go to great lengths to shave even an ounce off the

radio board weight. Some use carbon fiber and balsa laminates in an effort to build the lightest possible mounting surface. If it's not a racing hull, then suitably braced 1/16-inch to 1/8-inch plywood works. Reinforcement is needed to accommodate mounting screws for servos, switches, and winch mounting.

I prefer a tongue-and-screw mounting system where the front of the board has a projecting tongue that slides into a slotted cross member built into the hull. A blind 4-40 nut mounted on another cross member and a 4-40 bolt through the aft end of the radio board secure the board to the hull.

To remove the radio board, all that is necessary is to remove the sail winch arm and the single 4-40 bolt and slip the board out of the hull. (See figures 5-6A to 5-6C and 5-7A to 5-7B.)

Regarding receiver antenna routing, I lay the antenna right in the bottom of the hull. There doesn't seem to be any reason to bring the antenna above the deck. I have sailed several boats with as many different radios and have not lost control. Usually, when racing we stand within 10 feet of each other, and no one has reported any interference, cross talk, or loss of control.

The RC aircraft pilots occasionally report cross talk between channels as well as outside interference but it's never been a problem in the two clubs I sail with. The reason may be that our sailboats do not get as far out as the RC aircraft; therefore, the signal-to-noise ratio is not a problem even if there is outside interference. You can, if you prefer, run the receiver antenna up the backstay or mast.

Whether it's a kit or from scratch, when you build your boat it's a good idea to build up the radio board and get everything mounted on it before you put the deck on the hull. To avoid making the required hatch too big or too small, have the complete radio board on hand to determine the approximate length and width of the hatch opening. The ideal hatch opening is made as small as possible to minimize water entry.

The rudder servo and sail winch should be removable. To retain them I use No. 2 x 3/8-inch brass woodscrews. The receiver and battery pack are held in place with several rubber bands (strong enough to retain them but easy to remove for maintenance). I can change a battery pack quickly in the middle of a race day without even removing the radio board. This is important if you only have five minutes between heats. Figure 5-7 shows a radio board for a U. S. One Meter racing boat.

6

ALL ABOUT SAILS

Full-size sails come in all sizes and shapes. There are the more common Bermuda-sloop rigs, easily recognized by tall masts and triangular, high-aspect-ratio main and jib sail plans. Square-rigger sails are rectangular in shape. And there are the triangular, lateen sails seen today on sailboards like the Sunfish.

Another type is the gaff-rigged style, which uses a boom and an upper spar or boom known as a gaff from which the trapezoidal shaped sail is hung. Although not that common today, this type of sail plan was very common from the mid-1800s into the 1930s; it was gradually replaced by the more efficient Bermuda-sloop rig. Various sail plan types are shown in figure 6-1.

Each type of sail has had its day; and with the possible exception of the lateen sail, the Bermuda-sloop rig is the sail of choice today. This is due to its extremely high efficiency, particularly when going to windward.

Hard sails with their permanently molded shapes are on the leading edge of today's sail technology. With their trimmable luffs or leading edges, these sails are more efficient than the best Bermuda-rig fabric sails. However, to my knowledge this type of sail has not yet been seen in the model sailing community.

SAIL DYNAMICS

To understand how the sails actually drive the boat, let's turn to the basics of aerodynamics. The wind "pushes" the sails only when the boat is running downwind. When sailing into the wind, which sailboats do very well, the sails generate aerodynamic lift. To explain this, let's assume the boat is going to windward. The wind is directly out of the north, and we are sailing to the northwest, 45 degrees off the wind.

You might think this is impossible; figure 6-2 shows how it's actually done. The sail is constructed just like the wing of an aircraft. Although not as readily apparent, both broadseam-panelled sails and flat sails with a curved luff have a three-dimensional curved airfoil cross section. When the sail is trimmed to maximize the flow of air over the lee (convex curved) side of

the sail, a difference in atmospheric pressure is set up between the lee and windward (concave) sides of the sail. The high pressure on the lee side tries to equalize with the low pressure on the windward side. In doing so, a lifting force is created on the lee side of the sail that drives the boat forward.

Put another way, and as defined by Bernoulli, if the flow of air across the lee side of the sail is faster than the flow of air across the windward side (which it is), a low pressure area develops on the lee side of the sail. This difference in pressure between the two sides of the sail creates a lifting force that drives a model sailboat into the wind. When applied to a larger lifting area, this same force flies a fully loaded, 300,000-pound Boeing 747 into the air and keeps it there. It's a very practical demonstration of the axiom: nature abhors a vacuum.

The sails and keel work hand-in-hand: one balances the other, particularly when going to windward. Figure 6-3 shows the keel and sail force vectors that develop when the boat is sailed to windward.

NOTE: The actual wind direction is disregarded; as the boat moves forward, the sails only see the apparent wind. When the boat accelerates into the wind, the apparent wind direction rotates toward the bow of the boat. As the boat slows, the apparent wind moves aft. An easy way to see the direction of the apparent wind is to use cassette tape streamers taped to the mast head or shrouds.

The keel does three important things when the boat is sailing within 120 degrees of the wind:

1) Its lateral (side view) area resists the tendency of the boat to move sideways (that is, make leeway). Leeway is caused by the sail lift vector. This vector is not oriented in the same direction as the boat's line of travel. In fact, the lift vector may be 80 to 90 degrees to the right or left of the boat's actual line of travel. The keel area provides lateral resistance to the sideways force of the lift vector and converts some of the lift vector force into forward motion. Without the keel area, the boat simply would make leeway; it would not move forward at all.

2) The dead weight of the keel

under the hull provides a counterbalance or righting force to offset the heeling force generated by the sails' lift vector. Since the lift vector is virtually on the boat's beam and concentrated at the sails center of effort well above the deck, it doesn't take much wind to heel the boat when going to windward. As the boat heels, the amount of sail area exposed to the wind is reduced. As effective sail area is reduced, so is the heeling force. In the extreme case with the mast horizontal (boat knocked flat), the sail lift vector and heeling force are at zero, and the keel righting force is at maximum. The opposite is true when the boat is upright; heeling force is at maximum, and the keel righting moment is at zero. Like a seesaw, the two forces work in concert, one balances the other.

3) The keel generates a hydrodynamic lifting force that opposes the sail vector and reduces leeway. The lift is generated by the keel's symmetrical cross section as the boat moves to windward. The hull tends to point a little closer to the wind than its actual line of travel through the water. For example, the hull may be pointing at 40 degrees to the wind, but the actual course being sailed may be closer to 50 degrees to the wind. This angular difference produces different rates of water flow over the two sides of the keel. The difference in flow rates generates hydrodynamic lift just like the sails generate aerodynamic lift. The net effect at the keel is a lift vector located at 90 degrees to the centerline of the boat, which tries to push the boat back to windward. This offsets the sail lift vector that is trying to push the boat to leeward.

The three keel forces are most pronounced when going to windward and least evident when running off the wind. Only the ballast function is important when the boat is running straight downwind. The dynamics of sailing to windward may be summarized as being something like squeezing a wet pumpkin seed between your thumb and forefinger. The thumb represents the sail lift vector and the forefinger is the opposing keel lift vector. The force propelling the seed from between the two fingers is the resul-

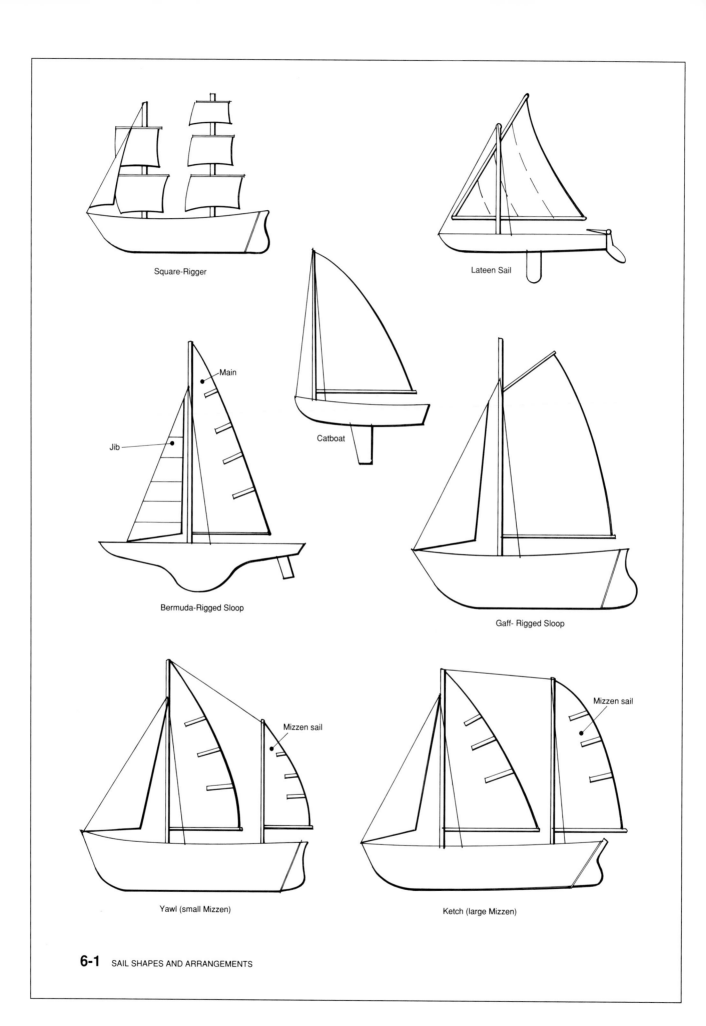

Square-Rigger

Lateen Sail

Main

Jib

Catboat

Bermuda-Rigged Sloop

Gaff- Rigged Sloop

Mizzen sail

Mizzen sail

Yawl (small Mizzen)

Ketch (large Mizzen)

6-1 SAIL SHAPES AND ARRANGEMENTS

tant sum of the opposing lift vectors.

Figure 6-4 shows the approximate sail settings for all points of sail. Incidentally, an easy way to practice rudder and sail control is to sail in a large circle just like the diagram shows. This technique will familiarize the neophyte skipper with the correct sail trim and term for each point of sail: running, beating, reaching, etc.

SAIL TERMINOLOGY, SELECTION, AND CONSTRUCTION

Before getting into actual sail construction, let's take a look at the proper terms for each part of the sail. This terminology can be a convenient shorthand means of communicating with other skippers and sailmakers. (It will also perpetuate the myth that sailboat people talk funny.)

Figure 6-5 identifies the standard main and jib sail terms—confusing at first, but frequent usage will fix that Also, see the glossary, page 62. In no time, you will be talking like one of the old salts!

Do note, however, the roach area for both main and jib. In most model racing classes this is a sort of free sail area allowed by the class rules. For a given class, if you are making your own sails, take as much roach area as you are allowed. More sail area provides more lift and consequently the boat goes faster.

In model boats, the main sail usually consists of five panels, all the same width. Panel seams usually run at right angles to the roach line. The jib, due to its somewhat smaller size, has only four panels. There is nothing sacred about the panel number; if you wish to experiment, go right ahead.

The sail's airfoil shape is locked permanently into the panels by broadseaming. As shown in figure 6-6, the individual sail panels are cut with almost imperceptible curves at their seams. When the panels are joined, the sail assumes a true three-dimensional airfoil cross section. Getting the right amount of broadseaming for a particular airfoil thickness is a delicate operation and may require more than one attempt. Today, even in the model sailmakers' lofts, computers calculate these curves.

An easier way to add fullness to the main sail (this won't work for the jib) is to use a one-piece, flat main sail with a slightly convex-curved luff. When the curved luff is attached to the mast, the luff curve forces fullness or belly into the sail. The exact amounts of broadseaming or luff curve are subjective and depend on the prevailing winds, the boat, and the skipper's personal experience and preference. A good rule of thumb: less is bet-

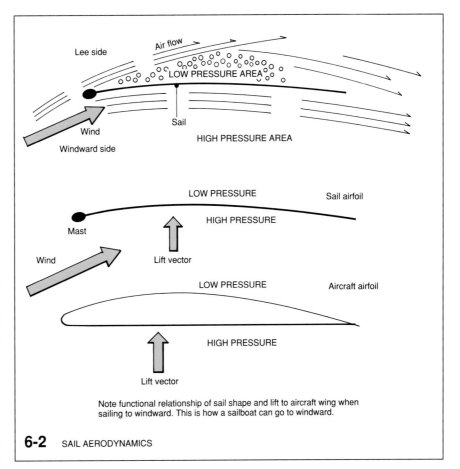

6-2 SAIL AERODYNAMICS

Note functional relationship of sail shape and lift to aircraft wing when sailing to windward. This is how a sailboat can go to windward.

ter. It's easy to add too much curve to the panels or luff.

When broadseaming panels, the adjoining panels must be joined accurately and smoothly right on the lines. There shouldn't be any wrinkles or puckers. If you use a luff curve for the main sail, it must be smooth and fair. Any deformities in sail shape upset the flow of air over the sail and reduce lift. It may take you several tries to produce a suit of sails that looks good and performs well.

It is precisely this challenge that many model skippers thrive on, particularly those who are relentlessly pursuing the great god of speed. Some racing skippers spend endless hours and effort to create the ultimate suit of sails. They see sailmaking as an opportunity to try new materials, shapes, and processes. And why not? There are plenty of materials to experiment with, and the costs are far less than commercial sails. Even the sails that don't turn out still teach the builder something. If nothing else, it's very good practice!

Each model skipper has a number of considerations to mull over when deciding just what kind of sails he's going to build or buy. If it's a racing class, he is restricted by the class rules that spell out maximum allowable sail area, luff height, roach

area, and the like. If he's building a scale boat, then he should try to stay close to the original sail dimensions.

Model skippers also need to consider the average wind speeds at the pond. Convenient design breaks are zero to 7 miles per hour, 8 to 15 miles per hour, and 16 miles per hour and up. Wind speeds determine the luff height, weight of the material, and the amount of broadseaming. Adjusting the length of the luff and foot of the sail and using different sail materials allow the sail designer to create a suit of sails for a particular set of weather conditions. Relatively flat sails are used in heavy air, and full sails are used in light air.

Storm sails have a shorter luff than standard sails and are used in heavy air to lower the center of effort, which reduces heeling when sailing to windward. Storm sails are permitted in some racing classes; in fact, certain classes allow up to three different suits of sails to be used. Storm sails also are used on scale boats, much like they are used in heavy weather on their full-size counterparts.

Sail material and weight give the sail designer additional options. Lighter materials are typically used for light air, while heavier materials are used for higher winds. Dacron, Composite Mylar, and Nylon synthetics are used almost exclusively today. Natural materials like cotton or silk are not used due to their porosity and tendency to rot and stretch when wet.

MAKING YOUR OWN SAILS

Making your own sails is not particularly difficult, but it does involve learning some new skills. If you are anything like me, your patience may be tried as you progress up the learning curve. Being used to working with solid materials like wood, plastic, and metals, I had to learn how to work with shapeless, formless material that at times seems to have a mind of its own.

The American Model Yacht Association has published several articles on sailmaking in their quarterly magazine, *Model Yachting*. Reprints are available through the AMYA. If you are serious about making your own sails, I strongly urge you to join the AMYA to take advantage of their reprint library and other information sources on sailmaking. (I won't describe the complete sailmaking process in detail here; the necessary text, photos, and drawings are beyond the scope of this book.)

There are several benefits when you make your own sails. You can make as many different suits as you need for varying wind conditions, your cost is very low, and you can experiment with new materials and broadseaming methods. If you are into scale boats, you may have to make your own since it might be the only way to get those special sails.

Sail material is available from several AMYA listed sources as well as your local sail loft. Lofts often give away or sell for a nominal fee leftover cuttings from full-size sails. The club I belong to has been using such materials for several years. We have used successfully Nylon spinnaker and Dacron sail material in several weights and colors. Most of this material has ripstop threads built in, which is important to prevent sail stretch. Cloth weights range from .5 ounce to 2.5 ounce. The .5-ounce cloth is a good all-around cloth to use on boats with total sail areas less than 800 squares.

Dacron of a 2.5-ounce weight is about the heaviest material you want to use for models. Generally speaking, the lighter the material, the better the sail shapes and holds its airfoil in light air. An excellent and readily available super lightweight material for racing is Coverite brand Micafilm. This material was designed to cover R/C airplanes. It does not have an iron-on adhesive coating on one side, making it perfect for our use. Its primary advantages are flexibility in light air,

6-3 KEEL AND SAIL FORCE VECTORS WHEN SAILING TO WINDWARD

durability, and low cost. You can purchase a 30-inch by 72-inch roll in a number of different colors for under $10. It should be available at your local hobby shop.

If nylon or Dacron is used, the entire sail can be cut from the same material. Micafilm by itself, however, does not have the inherent stiffness required for the trailing half of the sail. To maintain a smooth airfoil shape, it is necessary to use a heavier material like Dacron for the trailing 30 to 40 percent of the sail chord. Figure 6-7 shows a suit of sails for a U. S. One Meter boat purchased from Black Sails that uses a combination of lightweight Mylar (leading edge) and Dacron (trailing edge). The demarcation line is clearly visible in the photo. Note, too, the high-aspect-ratio of the sail plan. These sails work best in winds under 10 miler per hour.

Broadseaming is the most critical part of sailmaking. The laying out, cutting, and joining of the panels determines the performance potential of the sails. I use a 24-inch-long ship's

curve to draw the broadseaming curves for my sails. The high point of each chord or panel is set at 50 percent of the chord; using the ship's curve, a curved line is drawn from the high point to the luff and leech intersect points. The bottom panel gets the most curvature. I reduce progressively the height of each curve as the panels get smaller. The height of each chord is always in the same ratio to the length of each chord.

Prior to cutting material, it's a good idea to make a full-size paper pattern of each panel. Panel lines run at 90 degrees to the roach. The batten locations, panel overlap lines, and broadseaming curves are on the patterns. You can put five equal width panels in the main sail and four in the jib. All panels are broadseamed.

Depending on the sail area, typical panel overlap is from 3/16 inch to 1/2 inch. For example, the U. S. One Meter racing class with 600 square inches of sail area has a panel overlap of 3/16 inch to 1/4 inch. My largest boat has 900 square inches of sail and

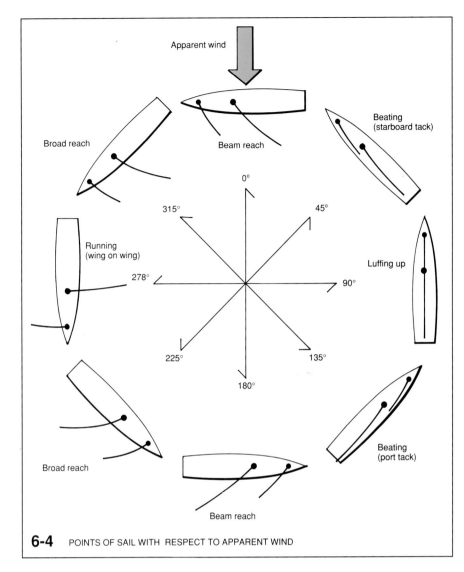

Apparent wind

Beam reach

Broad reach

Beating
(starboard tack)

0°

315°   45°

Running
(wing on wing)

Luffing up

278°   90°

225°   135°

180°

Broad reach

Beating
(port tack)

Beam reach

6-4   POINTS OF SAIL WITH RESPECT TO APPARENT WIND

1/2-inch panel overlaps. You can use the patterns to trace onto the sail material itself; this allows you to maximize material use. If you're like me, you will hoard a good piece of material until it's all gone.

Note that when cutting out the panels, you always leave an extra couple of inches of material beyond the luff and leech. You can lightly mark the luff and leech lines, but the panels are permanently joined before you cut the final luff and leech outlines.

When joining the panels, the luff line is used as a reference. Broadseams are smooth and fair. To join the panels, I like to use Coverite Balsarite. I sometimes will use 3M double-sided 1/2-inch tape. Generally, I prefer the Balsarite because it's easy to use, and the seams do not pucker when exposed to sunlight, which sometimes happens with the 3M tape.

I brush Balsarite onto the adjoining faces of each seam and wait until they are tacky. Then I join the panels, using a moderately hot iron. A seam never has come apart using this method even in the strongest blow. Of

course, it's a good idea to sew each seam once the panels are attached. The zigzag stitch works best.

Members of the AMYA are searching constantly for better double-sided tapes to use. The 3M tapes I use hold up well, but there is the pucker problem. Other double-sided tapes are available but not to the general public in small quantities. One local distributor had a 72-roll minimum order quantity!

The AMYA, however, does list tape brands and part numbers; perhaps you can find a roll in your area. If all you can find is 1/2 inch or wider, take it. A balsa stripper allows you to cut virtually any width you need from the roll.

If you are making one-piece flat sails (a good way to start), you can increase the draft of the main sail by adding the luff curve. The luff is cut with a slightly convex curve as shown in figure 6-8. When laying out this gentle curve, the sailmaker typically uses something like 1/8-inch to 1/4-inch of arc height for every 60 inches of luff length.

It does not take much luff curve to add too much fullness or draft to the main sail. This curve is never laid out on a panelled sail until after the panels are assembled. The assembled sail is pulled snug head-to-tack, and the luff curve is drawn using a flexible batten longer than the sail itself. The high point of this arc is about 45 percent up the sail from the tack. The curve is smooth and fair.

Mark the curve lightly on the sail material (I use a drafting pencil); an additional 1/4 inch to 1/2 inch of material also is lightly marked off, and the material cut on this line. The extra material is used as an overlap to retain a flexible wire running up the luff.

The jib luff is constructed in the same manner except the jib luff is cut straight rather than with a curve. Some skippers cut their jib luffs with an almost imperceptible amount of concave curve. This offsets the tendency of the jibstay to sag and distort in heavy air, which can reduce jib performance and efficiency.

Both the jib and main sail luff wires are terminated at the ends with small crimped eyes that become the attach points for the sails. The jib luff wire, when connected at both ends, becomes the jibstay. It interacts with the backstay: as the backstay tension is changed, the jibstay tension also changes. The skipper, using the backstay, actually changes the shape of the jib to improve boat speed.

The main sail is attached to the mast by means of a stranded wire jack line running up the backside of the mast. The jack line is held to the mast with small screw eyes or short pieces of brass tubing attached to the mast with epoxy or CYA-glued. Fishing leader stock makes good jack line material. The screw eyes are spaced every few inches from the gooseneck to the masthead. The jack line must be taut. The ends are terminated in eyes that are fastened to the masthead crane and bottom of the mast.

The tack end of the jibstay luff wire is attached to the jib boom or club, and the jib head end is attached to an adjustable line that runs to a fitting on the mast (see figure 6-9A). As an additional precaution, the jib tack grommet is also attached to the jib club; and another adjustable line is run from the jib head sail grommet to the same point on the mast. This allows the skipper to fine tune jib tension and shape.

The main sail is attached to the jack line with short pieces of .010 brass wire or nylon fishing line. Ties are made every couple of inches. An alternate method of attaching the main sail to the mast is by means of a

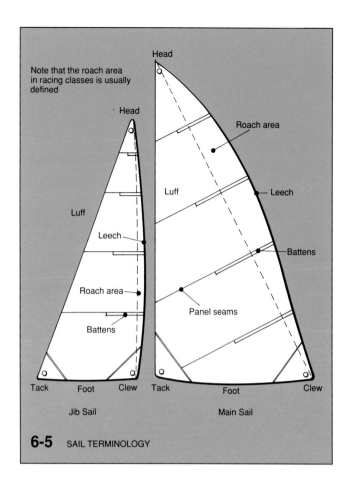

6-5 SAIL TERMINOLOGY

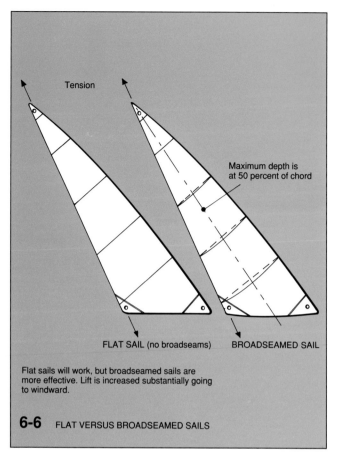

Flat sails will work, but broadseamed sails are more effective. Lift is increased substantially going to windward.

6-6 FLAT VERSUS BROADSEAMED SAILS

bolt rope sewn into the luff of the main sail. This method utilizes a groove in the aft side of the mast to retain the bolt rope. Weed Eater brand .090-inch line works well. Caution must be exercised when using this method, however, because of the sheer bulk of the bolt rope versus the stranded wire jack line. The sail luff material does not wrap as readily around the plastic line. Pop Up Mfg. sells extruded aluminum masts designed for use with a bolt rope.

Take care not to get puckers in the main sail luff. Unless you use one of Pop Up Mfg.'s extruded aluminum masts, you have to construct a mast with a built-in groove. This may result in a bulky and heavy mast.

The main and jib sail corners: clew, tack, and head (got those terms down yet?) are reinforced with sail material (called tabling) on both sides to stiffen the corners and reinforce the grommet attach points. The clews of both the jib and the main sails receive relatively large amounts of tabling. It's very important that the sail roach area from head to tack be smooth and flat with no tendency to curl.

Grommets are added to the three corners of each sail. I use a grommetting tool purchased at a local fabric store that came with an ample supply of plain brass and painted grommets. It does a neat job and should never wear out.

Battens are added to both jib and main sails to keep the trailing edges of the jib and main smooth and flat. On some boats (many catamarans and trimarans), the battens are full depth and the sails are almost rigid. Chinese junks are also like this. Battens are made easily from thin plastic such as .005-inch Styrene. If you build sails for an AMYA registered class boat, check the rules. Most class rules specify maximum batten length and the number allowed. Battens are attached with double-sided tape or Balsarite. Once in place, they are covered with lightweight strips of sail material.

COMMERCIAL SAILS

For those who prefer to buy rather than build their sails, there are several commercial sailmakers who can provide both standard and custom sails. Ballpark pricing for a suit of sails is currently in the $100 (600-square inches) to $175 range (1,200-square inches). Pricing varies depending on the materials you specify as well as other options such as bolt rope, grommets, colors, and so on.

The commercial sails I have seen were neatly constructed, held up well in heavy air, and, most importantly, were very competitive when raced. It's probably safe to say that the majority of racing skippers buy their sails.

Here is a short list of commercial sailmakers. You will find others listed in *Model Yachting Quarterly*.
• Hi-Perform Sails, 143 Kings Lake Rd., Willowdale, Ontario M2J3G
• Black Sails, 4761 Niagara Ave., San Diego, CA 92107
• Amen Design Group, 929 West St., Petaluma, CA 94952
• Rod Carr, 3011-177th Ave. NE, Redmond, WA 98052

SAIL ATTACHMENT AND ADJUSTMENT

After you acquire a suit of sails, attach them to the spars in such a way that ongoing adjustments can be made. Even with a super suit of sails, any skipper will have a problem if he can't tweak the sails pondside. Just about every attach point is adjustable on the well-rigged boat.

For example, the skipper needs to trim out excess weather helm by adjusting the rake of the mast and the jib sheet. This requires an adjustable backstay, jibstay, and jib sheet. Or he may have to change sail flatness with the clew outhaul to compensate for the weather that day. The boom vang and main sheet may need to be tweaked. The number of adjustments a skipper makes to improve boat performance and to compensate for the weather on any given day is almost infinite.

Figure 6-9B shows the sail adjustment and attach methods. By chang-

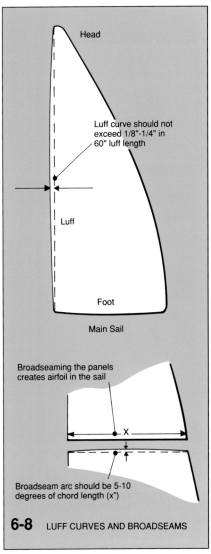

6-8 LUFF CURVES AND BROADSEAMS

Head

Luff curve should not exceed 1/8"-1/4" in 60" luff length

Luff

Foot

Main Sail

Broadseaming the panels creates airfoil in the sail

X

Broadseam arc should be 5-10 degrees of chord length (x")

Fig. 6-7. U.S. One Meter boat with a suit of sails by Black Sails. Note the different material weights: the leading half is thin, the trailing half relatively stiff. The corners are tabled (stiffened and reinforced).

ing the size of the fittings, these methods work for any size boat either scale or AMYA racing class. As you get started, no doubt you begin to develop your own methods. A trip to the local pond and close examination of the boats there will give you many stimulating ideas on how to put everything together and keep it that way.

PERFORMANCE AND TUNING

To improve boat speed, the skipper changes the sails' angle of attack and, to some extent, the draft of his sails. When going to windward, for example, the main and jib are sheeted in tight to get the main sail boom close to the deck centerline. This maximizes air flow over the main sail and allows the boat to sail as close as possible to the wind. As the boat shears off the wind, the skipper slacks the sails to keep them lifting and driving the boat at top speed.

When going to windward, take care that the boat does not heel excessively. Heeling looks impressive, but it actually slows the boat. If the lee rail is

awash, it's probably heeled too much. As the boat heels, the effective amount of sail area exposed to the wind is reduced, which slows the boat even more. The answer is to ease the sheets and come off the wind a bit. What looks like the longer route to the next mark actually takes less time because the boat is travelling faster.

Trying to sail too close to the wind is called pinching. Lift is a function of the angle of attack of the sails with respect to the apparent wind. The wise skipper constantly watches and trims his sails for signs that he is pinching and coming close to stalling the sails. Stalling breaks the flow of air across the sails. When stalled, the sails luff (or flap uselessly), and the boat is "dead in the water" until the skipper slacks the sails, gets the boat to fall off the wind, and eventually regains his way.

Don't get caught pinching in a race. If you do, the race is lost for sure. While you're struggling to "get out of irons," the rest of the fleet passes you by.

Depending on wind speed, the skipper adjusts the clew outhauls to increase or decrease sail flatness. A flattened sail works best on a windy day; in light air, it may not develop sufficient lift to drive the boat. The skipper loosens the clew outhauls to add fullness. This adjustment is somewhat analogous to switching from a super-thin, high-speed jet airfoil to a thick, slow-speed ultra-light airfoil.

Backstay tension also is used to control sail shape and jibstay tension either from shore or by servo on board the boat. Top racing skippers say backstay tension control is one of their most important adjustments.

The jib and the main sails act together to maximize lift and boat speed. It's possible to sail without a jib—just look at the New England catboats. However, by virtue of its ability to control the flow of air over the main sail, a jib allows the boat to point higher. When running straight downwind with the jib and main set wing-on-wing, the jib increases the effective amount of sail area.

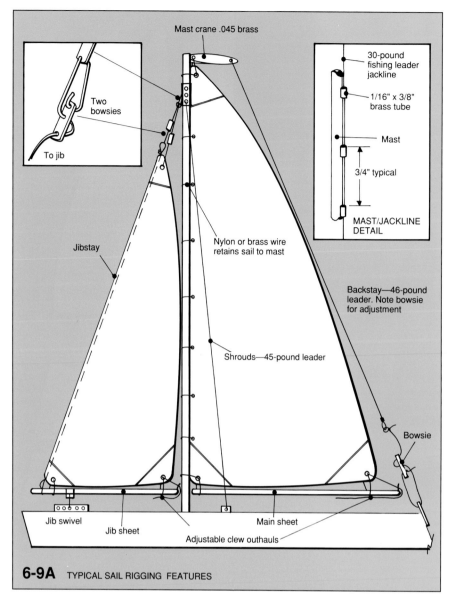

Mast crane .045 brass

Two bowsies

To jib

30-pound fishing leader jackline

1/16" x 3/8" brass tube

Mast

3/4" typical

MAST/JACKLINE DETAIL

Jibstay

Nylon or brass wire retains sail to mast

Backstay—46-pound leader. Note bowsie for adjustment

Shrouds—45-pound leader

Bowsie

Jib swivel

Jib sheet

Main sheet

Adjustable clew outhauls

6-9A TYPICAL SAIL RIGGING FEATURES

Fig. 6-10. A U.S. One Meter boat beating to windward. These sails are homemade from Dacron spinnaker cloth. They're cut a bit full and the jib club has lifted, causing the jib to belly too much. You can easily see the slot between the jib and main. It should always follow the same smooth curve top to bottom, and the sails should be roughly parallel as seen through the slot.

The jib acts much like the wing slats seen on many commercial aircraft. Anyone who flies in a Boeing or McDonnell-Douglas aircraft sees the leading edge wing slats deployed during the landing approach. The slats create a slot between the leading edge of the wing and the slat. The slot alters the flow of air over the leading edge of the wing to increase lift at slow air speeds.

The jib functions in the same way. By creating an adjustable slot between the main and the jib, the flow of air over the main is controlled. Not only does the jib control main sail lift, it also is used to increase or decrease weather helm. (See figure 6-10 for a good picture of the slot.)

As a rule of thumb, when setting the jib with respect to the main sail, the jib extends approximately 5 degrees further out than the main at all sail settings, from closehauled to all the way out. The jib never is sheeted in more than the main. The slot is roughly parallel from head to foot with no sail wrinkling or distortion at any point.

REFERENCE MATERIAL

The AMYA has an excellent collection of sail articles and reprints covering methods of sail construction, tuning, rigging, and sail aerodynamics.

The local library is also a good source. Most stock a wide variety of books on sailing, including sailmaking, racing, trimming, and tactics. Much of this material can be readily adapted as is.

Fig. 6-9B. Rigging detail: the adjustable jib club-to-deck attach point. The jib club must be adjustable fore and aft and it must always pivot freely. You can use backstay adjustments to control jib tension.

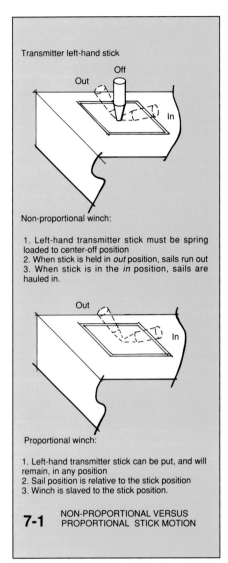

Off

Out

In

Non-proportional winch:

1. Left-hand transmitter stick must be spring loaded to center-off position
2. When stick is held in *out* position, sails run out
3. When stick is in the *in* position, sails are hauled in.

Out

In

Proportional winch:

1. Left-hand transmitter stick can be put, and will remain, in any position
2. Sail position is relative to the stick position
3. Winch is slaved to the stick position.

7-1 NON-PROPORTIONAL VERSUS PROPORTIONAL STICK MOTION

7

SAIL WINCHES

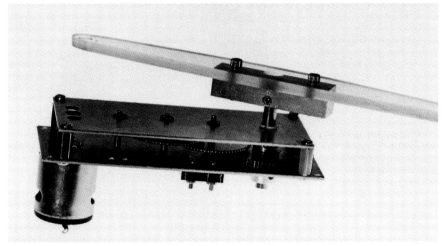

Fig. 7-2. Dumas No. 3601 non-proportional winch. A servo controlled DPDT switch is required to reverse winch rotation. This is a powerful winch suitable for larger boats over 1000-square inches of sail area.

The sail winch plays an extremely important role in controlling the sailboat. Without a winch, the boat's ability to perform is handicapped severely. The sail winch sets your sails exactly where you want them. On a full-size boat, sail trim is crucial to its speed and efficiency. The skipper constantly monitors and adjusts sail trim to maximize boat speed and hold the desired heading. Wind speed and direction are rarely constant; to simply hold a heading, the skipper constantly feeds in small trim corrections as the wind velocity and direction change.

The winch is an absolute necessity when bringing the boat about from a downwind run to a beat into the wind or vice versa. Without it, the skipper is not able to pull in the sheets to sail closehauled. Nor can he pay out the

sheets when coming about from a beat to a reach or run. The sail winch lets you quickly trim the sails as needed just as if you were on board.

Another useful feature of winch-controlled sails is the ability to steer the boat without using the rudder. Use the rudder to turn the boat, but never to maintain the boat's direction. Sailing this way causes rudder drag and consequent speed penalty. Once turned to a new heading, the smart skipper keeps the rudder centered and uses the winch to hold the new lay line. For example: to move the bow further off the wind, ease the sheets slightly; to swing the bow further into the wind or point higher, pull the sheets in slightly. These sail trim changes also increase boat speed.

The wind is rarely constant. In one

afternoon of sailing, you may encounter wind shears, dead air, heavy air, and sudden puffs. These changes demand immediate attention to the sails. Sailing into a puff or shear can lay a boat on its beam ends if the skipper doesn't get the sails slacked in time. An experienced skipper keeps one eye on the sails and the other on the wind and water. He uses many different sail settings and very little rudder input. After sailing models for awhile, this sort of thing will become automatic.

The winch sets the sails at any point from closehauled (main boom over the deck centerline) to fully slacked (main boom against the shrouds) and is powerful enough to haul in the sails in winds up to 25 miles per hour. It must be fast enough

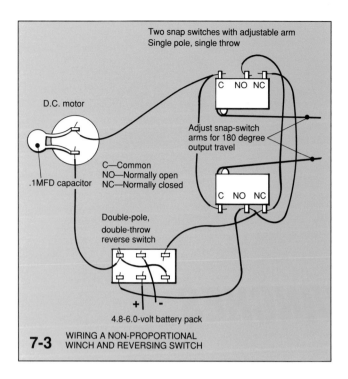

7-3 WIRING A NON-PROPORTIONAL WINCH AND REVERSING SWITCH

Two snap switches with adjustable arm
Single pole, single throw

D.C. motor

.1MFD capacitor

Adjust snap-switch arms for 180 degree output travel

C—Common
NO—Normally open
NC—Normally closed

C NO NC

C NO NC

Double-pole, double-throw reverse switch

+   −

4.8-6.0-volt battery pack

so you won't lose your position in the fleet each time you retrim the sails if you are racing.

As each mark is rounded in a race, you must retrim the sails. For example, when coming about from a beat to a broad run, the sails must be eased quickly. The rate at which the sails are retrimmed by the winch is crucial to maintaining boat speed. There isn't much stored momentum in a light racing hull; the faster the sails are slacked, the less energy is lost and the faster the boat accelerates onto its new heading.

On a scale or non-racing model, winch speed is less critical. A slow-moving winch works just fine. Note that when we talk about winch speed,

we are referring to the transit time of the winch arm, or the time it takes for the arm to swing through its full arc. Two to three seconds full travel under load is considered good. Winch transit time is measured under load; running it no-load in your garage or without the sails attached doesn't mean a thing.

Also consider the output rating of the winch. There are two criteria to consider: output torque (which is expressed in inch-ounces) and the number of square inches of sail area that the winch is rated to haul in. Sail area and average windspeeds in your area dictate the torque you will need.

The lightest and smallest commercial winch I know of is the Futaba S-25 proportional sail servo rated at something less than 100 inch-ounces and suitable for up to 600 square inches of sail area. Depending on wind speed, transit time is two to three seconds. Airtronic manufactures a somewhat larger proportional sail servo, the Model 94581. It handles up to 800 squares. In lighter air, it handles up to 900 squares. Due to its higher output torque, its transit time is longer than the Futaba S-25.

The most powerful winches I know of are the Dumas 3701 non-proportion-

al and 3703 proportional models (The terms proportional and nonproportional winch are defined a bit further on in this chapter). Both are rated at something over 600 inch-ounces with transit times of around five seconds. The Dumas winches easily haul in over 1,000 square inches of sail.

Victor also has a heavy-duty nonproportional winch that is suitable for boats with up to 1,200-square-inch sail areas. This winch is used in a J-Boat, the largest of the AMYA racing classes. The trade-off of course, is that it's a pretty heavy and bulky winch. But in a J-Boat this isn't a problem.

The Futaba, Airtronic, Dumas, and Victor winches are available through hobby stores and direct mail firms.

Generally, one winch is used to simultaneously control the main and the jib sails. A two-channel radio is used: one channel for winch control and the other for rudder control. For the ultimate in sail control, two independently controlled winches are used: one for the main and the other for the jib. This configuration requires a three-channel radio. (Two-winch sail control isn't covered in this book. For the neophyte skipper, independent sail control adds little to performance, is difficult to install, and requires an experienced skipper to fully utilize its potential.)

WINCH TYPES

There are two kind of sail winches: nonproportional and proportional. The basic difference between the two is that the nonproportional winch runs in one direction or the other as long as the transmitter stick is held full-up or full-down from the spring-loaded center position. The proportional winch moves to whatever stick position is selected and stops. If the stick is

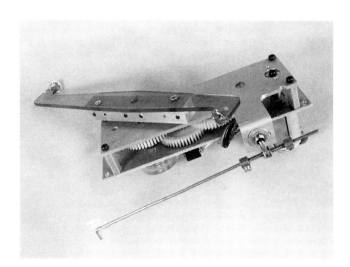

Fig. 7-4A. Another non-proportional winch, this one was built from scratch by by Rolf Andersen. Note the DPDT motor-reversing switch and pushrod.

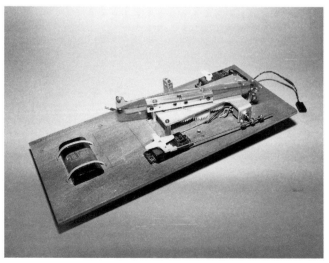

Fig. 7-4B. Rolf Andersen's homemade winch installed on the radio board. The receiver is underneath.

moved 50 percent of its travel, the winch arm also moves 50 percent and stops. The proportional stick does not have a spring-loaded center position. An internal ratchet prevents inadvertent stick motion and consequent winch output arm movement. The relationship of stick movement to winch position is shown in figure 7-1.

NON-PROPORTIONAL WINCHES

In general, the nonproportional winch delivers more torque than its proportional counterpart. (An exception to this is the Dumas 3603 proportional model.) However, to paraphrase a basic physics law, you don't get something for nothing, and winches are no exception. Higher torques mean more weight and often greater bulk. Stronger motors with greater amp draws and additional reduction gear sets must be used to provide the higher output torques. And the stronger winch will have slower transit times.

The extra weight is a blessing in a scale model where you need additional ballast in the bilges. In the smaller boat racing classes, however, the weight is not welcome. Generally, local skippers who race a particular class can tell you what winch works best in a class. In scale boats, winch size is not critical as long as there is sufficient torque to haul in the sails.

To provide high torque, the nonproportional winches rely on a high gear reduction ratio between the motor and the output shaft. Swapping speed for torque, these winches provide plenty of power but at a very low rate of speed. Consequently, the output arm moves very slowly and results in slow trim changes. This is a problem for the racing skipper. Unless all boats in the fleet are equipped with this same slow winch, this winch is at a serious disadvantage when rounding the marks. While the others retrim and accelerate away toward the next mark, the boat with the slower winch is still retrimming and trying to get under way.

Figure 7-2 shows the Dumas 3601 nonproportional winch. The 3603 proportional model uses the same motor and gear train but has an added feedback pot and electronic circuit for proportional control.

Nonproportional winches use an instant-reversing, permanent-magnet, D.C. motor rated at 2.4 to 7.2 volts. The motor drives a heavy-duty gear train that is coupled to a vertical output shaft. The motor runs in both directions; direction of rotation is controlled by a double-pole, double-throw (DPDT), center-off reversing switch. When the motor is energized, the gear train rotates the output shaft and output arm. The reversing switch sets motor polarity which, in turn, controls

Fig. 7-5. The Airtronic No. 94581 proportional sail winch is suitable for sail areas up to 800-square inches. The output arm can be extended if necessary.

Fig. 7-6. The Futaba S-25 proportional sail winch is suitable for sail areas up to 600-square inches of sail area.

the direction of output arm rotation.

A standard R/C aircraft servo controls the position of the double-pole, double-throw reversing switch. Both toggle and slide DPDT switches are used. These are available from Radio Shack and other electronic outlets. Any switch rating works.

Output arm travel doesn't exceed 180 degrees. More than that reduces sail travel and fouls the lines. Limit switches on the output shaft sense the output arm position and stop the motor at the end of the desired arc. Commercially available winches usually include everything you need

except the DPDT, center off reversing switch, and servo. You may have to cut the output arm to length to suit your boat. The limit switch arms are bent to get 180 degrees of travel.

Figure 7-3 shows a typical wiring diagram for a nonproportional winch. Some fiddling with the two end-of-travel limit switches is required in order to get the arm to rotate exactly 180 degrees. Sheet routing through the winch is shown further along in this chapter.

You may want to build your own nonproportional winch. Figures 7-4A and 7-4B show such a winch built by

Rolf Andersen for a U. S. One Meter boat that performed well for three racing seasons. It uses two 1.2 volt-nicads in series for power and has no trouble sheeting in 600 squares. With a 4.8-volt battery, it could handle much more sail area. The upper and lower plates are aluminum while the gears are nylon running in brass bushings. There are four stages of reduction. The overall reduction ratio is 15:1. The motor came from an Oster electric clipper and the gears from an Oster electric can opener. The output arm is acrylic plastic with brass eyes for the sheet guides. The DPDT, center-off reversing switch and its push-pull link to the reversing servo are clearly shown. Note the spring-loaded, override feature Rolf built into the servo-to-switch link.

Others have adapted small plastic three-stage gear motors found at electronic surplus houses. Some of these have plastic gears, others have brass gears. Any gear ratio from about 10:1 to 20:1 ought to work. Motor speed and torque are increased by increasing the voltage to the motor. There are plenty of low-cost gear motors available for conversion to nonproportional winches for the experimentally minded and cost-conscious model shipwright.

When using nonproportional winches, it's best to separate the winch battery from the receiver battery. In other words, don't use the receiver battery to power the winch. The standard receiver battery is rated at 500-milliamperes per hour (mah) capacity. The winch drains this rather quickly on a windy day and can leave you circling helplessly in the middle of the pond with no receiver power. Either nicads or dry cells are used for winch power. I prefer the nicads because I'm always sure of their charge state. A heavy-duty winch like the Dumas 3601 should have a separate 4.8-volt battery rated at 1,200 mah.

The winch output arm hauls in or slacks the sheets. To get the sails positioned where you want them with a nonproportional winch, the transmitter stick momentarily is held in the full-up or full-down position. This places the reversing switch servo arm at one end of its travel, which moves the DPDT reversing switch toggle from its center-off position to either the foward or reverse position. The motor runs in the direction selected by the reversing switch. The winch output arm rotates in the direction selected at the transmitter.

Moving the transmitter stick to the opposite position reverses the sequence; the output arm rotates in the opposite direction. Holding the stick in the full-up position slacks the sheets; in the full-down position the sheets are hauled in. Returning the stick to the center neutral position centers the DPDT switch and stops winch rotation.

Stopping the sails exactly where you want them can be tedious; depending on the speed of the winch and wind speed, you may have to jog the stick to ease the sails into their proper trim. After a while, this kind of sail control becomes instinctive: up-stick equals sails out and down-stick equals sails in!

The standard convention in RC sailing is to use the left-hand stick for sail control and the right-hand stick for rudder. This avoids a lot of confusion when sailing a different boat. The other convention is: left-stick up always slacks the sails, and left-stick down hauls them in.

When using a nonproportional winch, the transmitter left-stick must be spring loaded to the center position. This is not a problem; all the inexpensive two-channel radios come this way for use with R/C cars.

PROPORTIONAL WINCHES

Proportional winches perform the same basic function as their nonproportional brethren. They are installed on the radio board and the sheets are rigged just like the nonproportional models. Their difference lies in the

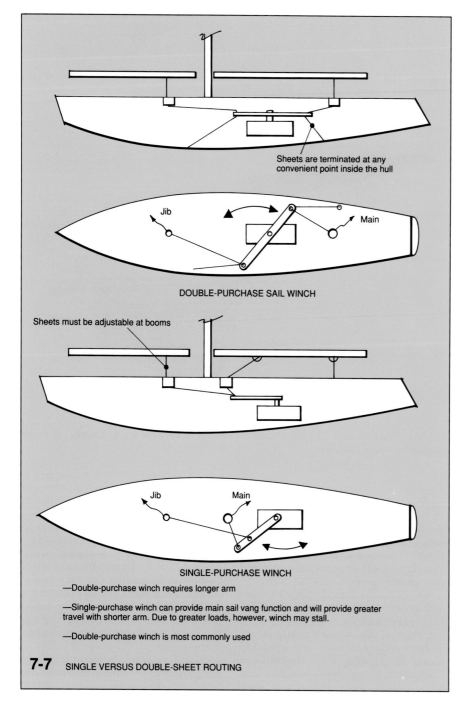

Sheets are terminated at any convenient point inside the hull

Jib   Main

DOUBLE-PURCHASE SAIL WINCH

Sheets must be adjustable at booms

Jib   Main

SINGLE-PURCHASE WINCH

—Double-purchase winch requires longer arm

—Single-purchase winch can provide main sail vang function and will provide greater travel with shorter arm. Due to greater loads, however, winch may stall.

—Double-purchase winch is most commonly used

7-7   SINGLE VERSUS DOUBLE-SHEET ROUTING

fact that they are really just over-grown servos that deliver much more torque than their smaller R/C aircraft cousins. Unlike the nonproportional winch, this winch plugs directly into the receiver. Since it receives its power and signal commands from the receiver, the DPDT reversing switch, reversing switch servo, and winch battery required for the nonproportional winch are eliminated.

Getting rid of these components saves several ounces of weight and reduces the size of the radio board. But you must remember that the winch draws all its power from the receiver battery. You have to make sure your receiver battery has the ampere-hour capacity to sustain a couple hours of windy day sailing. Even the relatively low current draw Futaba S-25 proportional sail winch aboard a 600-square-inch boat can drain a 500-mah battery in an hour of windy day sailing.

If you are going to use a 500-mah battery pack in winds over 10 miles per hour, bring an extra fully-charged battery pack to the pond, and switch to it after the first hour. A good rule of thumb for 500-mah battery packs: if the average windspeed is under 10 miles per hour, you can use the same battery pack for two hours of actual sailing time. If windspeed is over 10 miles per hour, plan on switching after an hour of actual sailing time. (Here in Wisconsin, 25 mile-per-hour winds are fairly common.) If you can afford the luxury of more weight, an 800-mah or higher rated battery pack is very good insurance. On larger boats, that are 50 inches and longer, you should plan on using a 1,200-mah pack. All receiver battery packs are rated at 4.8 volts; only the mah rating changes.

There are several proportional sail winches available. In order of descending torque rating, you can choose from the Dumas model 3603, Airtronic model 94581 (figure 7-5), and the Futaba S-25 (figure 7-6). In addition to these, giant scale aircraft servos from Airtronic, Futaba and World Engines are easily modified to sail winch duty. These giant scale servos, intended for use on R/C aircraft with 72-inch to 108-inch wingspans, easily handle 600-square-inch sail areas. For boats with less than 600 squares, standard-sized R/C aircraft servos are used. When using aircraft servos, an extended arm is bolted to the original servo arm. The new arm is cut from .045-inch aluminum or 3/32-inch acrylic plastic.

The proportional winch consists of a D.C. micro-motor, gear train, and tiny printed circuit board assembly enclosed in a plastic case. Incidentally, this case is usually not watertight.

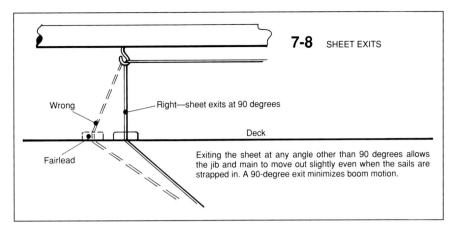

7-8 SHEET EXITS

Wrong

Right—sheet exits at 90 degrees

Deck

Fairlead

Exiting the sheet at any angle other than 90 degrees allows the jib and main to move out slightly even when the sails are strapped in. A 90-degree exit minimizes boom motion.

The p. c. board circuit and a shaft-mounted potentiometer control the motor and the shaft position. The p. c. circuit receives its instructions from the receiver; the circuit controls motor run time and direction of rotation. The position potentiometer on the output shaft tells the receiver when the output shaft has reached the desired position; the circuit then shuts off the motor.

The receiver gets its commands from the transmitter left-hand stick movement. The receiver, sail and rudder servos, and the transmitter are a closed-loop servo system. The proportional sail winch and rudder servo are slaved to the left-hand and right-hand transmitter sticks, respectively. In fact, the word servo is derived from the Latin noun servus (slave) and the verb servo (to serve).

The closed-loop servo concept is not new. It dates back to World War II where similar but more powerful servos and electron tube circuits were used on aircraft to remotely control cowl flaps, elevator, aileron, rudder trim, and gun aiming from the cockpit. Functionally, the only significant difference between those systems and the systems used today is that the World War II servo commands travelled by wire from the cockpit to the servo. Today's systems utilize AM, FM, and pulse-width-modulated (pwm) signals sent from the transmitter to the receiver.

To demonstrate how the system works, let's assume that you move the left-hand transmitter stick from its lowest position up to the mid-point position. As you do this, a potentiometer on the stick measures the amount of stick movement. The new stick position is encoded and sent to the receiver. The signal is sent in the form of a digital pulse-train and is modulated onto the transmitter AM, FM, or pwm carrier frequency.

The receiver decodes this information and compares it to the position of the potentiometer on the output shaft

of the winch. Since the transmitter potentiometer position does not match the winch potentiometer position, the receiver runs the winch motor in the direction specified by the new transmitter potentiometer position. The receiver runs the winch motor until the winch potentiometer position matches the transmitter potentiometer position. When they are matched, the system is nulled (balanced); the receiver stops the winch motor and output arm in the new position.

The servo is set to operate like the nonproportional winch: moving the stick up slackens the sails, moving the stick down hauls them in.

The proportional winch replicates the tiniest amount of transmitter stick motion. The system is linear, and moving the transmitter stick halfway through its travel positions the winch at the midpoint of its travel.

In most cases, the proportional winch servo has faster transit time than a nonproportional winch. By simply checking stick position on the transmitter, the skipper can always tell approximately where his sails are positioned. This can be a plus when the boat is 100 yards away and sail position is not readily apparent.

So, why doesn't everyone use proportional winches? The fact is that for larger boats about the only proportional winch available strong enough to handle the sail areas required is the Dumas 3603. Some skippers prefer to scratchbuild, and a nonproportional winch is much easier to build than a proportional one. Because of their associated electronics, proportional winches are considerably more expensive—particularly the larger, more powerful winches.

Personally, I prefer to use proportional winches. While they may cost more, the weight-saving aspect and smaller size are more important to me than cost. However, most of my focus is on racing and speed where weight and bulk are critical. In a scale or sport class boat, you can use either

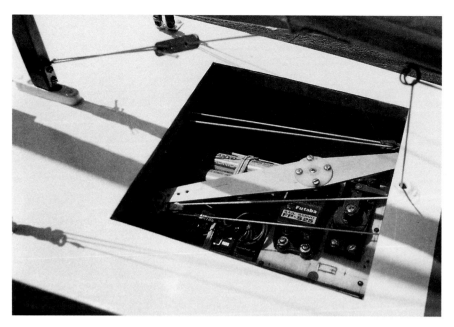

Fig. 7-9. To reduce winch loading and consequent heavy battery drain, minimize friction at the sheet guides and exits. In this U.S. One Meter boat, small brass pulleys reduce friction where the sheets pass through the ends of the winch output arm.

type; it won't make a bit of difference. If you decide you want independent jib and main sail control, you have to plan on using proportional winches. I don't know of any easy way to independently control jib and main with two nonproportional winches. You would need two winch radio channels plus the rudder channel and some means by which to pulse both winch channels.

RIGGING THE WINCH

The winch arm position controls the sail settings. Lines (or sheets as they are correctly called) run from attach points on the main sail boom and jib club to or through the ends of the winch output arm. As the output arm rotates through its arc in response to the transmitter commands, the arm either hauls in or slacks the sheets. Closehauled, the main sail boom is positioned close to the centerline of the deck. Conversely, with the sheets fully slacked, the main sail boom rests against the shrouds. The jib club in the closehauled position should match the main sail boom position. With the sheets fully slacked, the jib club is swung out 90 to 95 degrees from the centerline of the boat.

There are two basic methods for rigging the sheets: single and double purchase. Both methods are shown in figure 7-7. The basic difference is that you get more sail travel with the double purchase method, but either the sheets are located further out on the boom and jib club or a longer winch arm is necessary. In my opinion, the double purchase method is more popular, but either method works.

There are three variables to consider when routing and connecting the sheets. The sheets control the amount of sail travel with respect to the output arm motion. Your goal is to get the main sail boom to move from the centerline and to rest against the shrouds as the winch output arm rotates from one end of its arc to the other. If you are contemplating a kit boat, this geometry is worked out for you already. If you are building from plans or from your own design, read on.

The first thing to determine is the length of the winch output arm. It should be as long as possible and still fit crosswise in the hull. As you swing the output arm through its arc, make sure that the arm does not strike the interior of the hull. If this happens, you limit travel as well as jam the winch causing excessive locked rotor current draw that destroys the winch motor. When you do this, take into account that the main sail end of the arm is probably longer than the jib end. The pivot point is not at the midpoint of the arm. The winch has to be offset from the hull centerline to accommodate the longer main sail arm end.

The second thing is to set the arm travel from closehauled to fully slacked. Make it 180 degrees or a bit less. This is done by adjusting the end-of-travel limit switches on the nonproportional winch. On a proportional system, the transmitter stick trim is used to increase travel as required.

The attach point locations on the main boom and jib club are the third consideration. The sheet attach point

is moved toward the mast to get more main boom travel and away from the mast for less travel. On the jib club, the opposite holds true: the connection point is moved away from the mast for more travel and toward the mast for less travel.

You'll find in short order that the sheet rigging process is a juggling act to get the right amount of sail travel while adjusting the three variables. If you change one of the three variables, you change the other two.

First of all, make the output arm as long as possible. Secondly, maximize output arm travel up to 180 degrees. The crosswise position of the arm in the hull determines its overall length. The arm travel on a nonproportional winch is easily set to 180 degrees by bending the end-of-travel limit switch arms. On a proportional system, you'll get 120 to 130 degrees of travel with the transmitter stick motion and another 20 to 30 degrees of travel with the trim lever.

The proportional system is set up so that the sails are strapped in when the left-hand stick and the trim lever are full-down. The sails are fully slacked with the left-hand stick and trim lever in their full-up positions. Final adjustments are made at the main boom and jib club attach points using bowsies that give you another 5 to 10 degrees of adjustment.

The easiest way to set up the sheet routings and connection points is to do so before the deck is installed. I start by installing the radio board in its final location (usually right at the center of buoyancy). A temporary 1/8-inch by 1/2-inch pine or basswood output arm with a row of 1/16-inch holes drilled in both ends is attached to the winch. This arm is only a substitute for the final arm that is patterned after the dummy. I make the pivot hole in the arm just large enough to slip over the winch output shaft. The dummy arm pivots freely, but it does not actually drive or position the sails. We'll use the Armstrong method for now.

With the radio board in place and the dummy arm mounted on the winch, I temporarily set the mast, boom, and jib club in place. Since there are no shrouds or stays yet and nowhere to attach them, I tie the top of the mast to a convenient point (a hook screwed into an overhead floor joist). I level the hull and vertically locate the mast just about where its going to end up. It doesn't really matter for this exercise if the mast is off a couple of degrees in any direction.

The sails are not needed yet. If you have them, fine; but if you do not, masking tape is used to hold the main boom and jib club parallel to the deck.

The king plank, which is the main support member running the length of the hull under the deck, should be in place at this time to locate the sheet exit guides.

I always start with the dummy arm in the closehauled or fully sheeted position. In this position, the arm is pointing fore and aft with the main sail end pointing at the bow. I use this convention on all of my boats; close-hauled, the main sail end points to the bow and the jib end points to the stern. These positions are reversed when the sails are fully let out.

Temporary sheets are run through their respective holes in the ends of the output arm and up through holes drilled in the king plank about where I think the sheets should exit. The other ends of the sheets are tied to small eyes screwed into the interior of the hull. Locate them as shown in figure 7-8. When you locate the main sheet exit point, make sure it's not going right through your future access hatch location. The main sheet exit should be aft of this hatch.

With the arm rotated to the close-hauled position and the sheets threaded through the king plank, the main boom and jib club are positioned over the deck centerline. The sheets are taped to the boom and club directly above their respective exit points. To verify these attach points, I slowly rotate the output arm by hand from the closehauled position to the fully slacked position. As the arm moves, the sheets slacken and allow the sails to move away from the hull. Ideally, the main boom stops about where the shrouds eventually are attached, and the jib club stops at 90 to 95 degrees to the centerline of the hull. In reality, this never happens on the first try.

If the sails don't go out far enough, the sheet attach points should be repositioned until they do. It's a tedious process of adjusting and checking sail position at both ends of the arm travel. Eventually, you will find the boom, arm, and sheet exit combination that work. Each time you change the boom and club attach points, you rethread the sheets through another set of holes in the king plank to keep the sheets vertically oriented as they exit the king plank.

The sheets must exit vertically through the deck and never at an angle. An angular exit allows the sails to move away from the hull when sailing closehauled. This prevents you from really strapping in your sails tight and windward performance suffers. Figure 7-9 shows the main sheet exit and friction-reducing pulleys on a U. S. One Meter boat.

With the sheet attach points

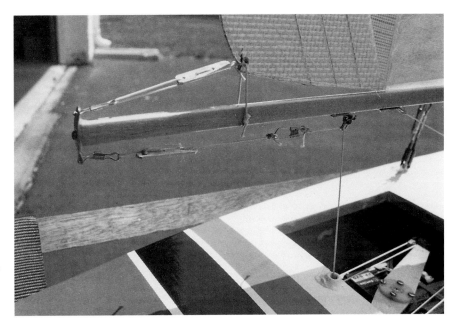

Fig. 7-10. Jib and main sail sheets must be adjustable to independently trim the sails and set them when the winch is sheeted in hard. A simple bowsie works well—there should be at least one to two inches of adjustment in each sheet.

marked on the boom and club and the sheet exits located on the king plank, you install the deck. You use 1/8-inch i.d. brass or nylon eyelets or fairleads as sheet exit guides on the deck. To reduce sheet friction on the underside of the king plank, I usually install the same eyelets under the king plank as well. Others use small blocks or pulleys below decks to route the sheets from the winch arm up through the deck to the boom and jib club.

Rod Carr, an old AMYA hand and master sailmaker, gave me the idea of locating the sheet exits before the deck is installed. Until Rod wrote up his method in *U. S. Boat & Ship Builder*, I always located the sheet exits after the deck was in place. It's a lot easier to do it Rod's way.

If a light winch like the Futaba S-25 is used on windy days, sail pressure and resultant sheet friction may prevent the winch from really strapping in the sails. The friction occurs at the deck exits and the output arm. Small, nylon no-snag pulleys are available from Pop-Up Mfg. Proctor also manufactures a line of suitable, small brass pulleys. Either type reduces friction and high-amp draw at the winch. The pulleys are tied loosely to the ends of the winch arm so that they can move somewhat as the winch arm rotates through its arc. Figure 7-9 shows Proctor brass pulleys attached to the output arm of a Futaba S-25 winch installed in a U. S. One Meter boat.

At the points where the sheets attach to the boom and jib club, some kind of adjustment is needed to permit

sheet trim at the pond. One to two inches of adjustment is sufficient. Sheet trim is necessary to permit the skipper to respond to wind speed changes, sheet stretch, and small variations in winch travel. This is done easily by adding a bowsie to each sheet as shown in figure 7-10.

For the sheets, I use 20-pound test, braided fly-fishing line with no problems. I like this stuff because it doesn't slip easily through a bowsie and make inadvertent line adjustments at the wrong time! You also can use monofilament fishing line or other nylon and Dacron lines that you can find at the surplus outlets.

Use whatever you like; just be sure it withstands at least a 20-pound pull test, won't stretch when wet, and is capable of having knots tied in it that won't come apart. Also watch for chafing at output arm and exit guide points. I had problems with some nylon lines that were strong enough but that frayed at the deck exits and eventually broke. The braided fly-fishing line I use never does this, and it's available at any well-stocked fishing store. Monofilament seems to work well, but you must be careful when tying knots because they can come undone.

Hopefully, this gives you the impetus to get out there and build or buy that all-important sail winch. As I mentioned earlier, you can wander around a pond without a winch; but you are not really the skipper of your boat until you can order both rudder and sail changes. Now that's sailing!

8
RACING

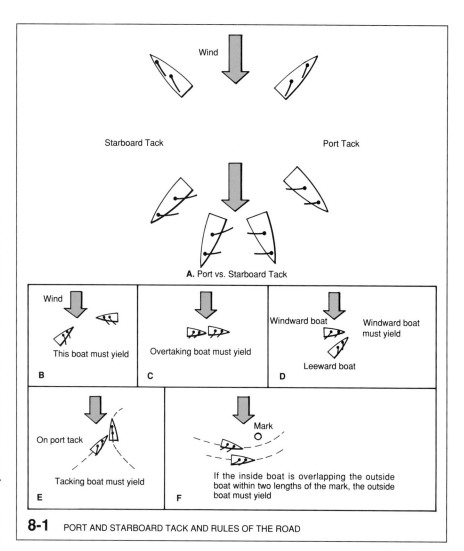

8-1 PORT AND STARBOARD TACK AND RULES OF THE ROAD

It doesn't matter whether you match sail (two identical boats one-on-one) or enter a regatta (where there may be up to twelve boats in a single heat), racing is always exciting. And since the boats are all in the same class or otherwise handicapped in some way, it usually comes down to skipper skill.

Expensive, go-fast Kevlar hulls are available, as well as super-light carbon fiber spars and commercially made sails and the finest sail winch money can buy. However, this package is likely to cost in excess of $1,000! But money won't buy you any wins if you lack the skills developed by practicing virtually every weekend against the best competition you can find. It's a fact that a top skipper can win races with a mediocre boat, but an unskilled skipper does not win regardless of what boat he sails.

Do your homework and learn how to tune your boat for maximum speed in a given set of weather conditions. Otherwise, stay with an inexpensive, well-designed kit like the Victor Soling or Amen Infinity 54 and practice, practice, practice. It also helps to talk to the skippers who are winning. Ask them what they do to make their boats go faster. Our club has had several programs presented by winning skippers on tuning, tactics, and sailmaking. If these people won't share their knowledge with new skippers, you're probably in the wrong club.

Anyone coming into racing soon finds out there are plenty of items available to help your boat go faster, handle better, and aid reliability. The type of hardware to buy largely depends on what AMYA classes, if any, are raced in your area. The Marblehead class, for example, is a development class aimed at very fast boat speeds. There is probably more go-fast, add-on hardware available for this class than any other. You can spend a lot of money on a Marblehead; to be competitive in this class, you may have to.

At the same time, if you don't want to participate in an active racing class, start a beginner's one-design class using the Kyosho Fairwind, Victor Soling, Amen Infinity 54, or whatever

the club happens to have at the time. Our club selected the U. S. One Meter class because we liked its size, and we wanted to start a club scratchbuilding project. It turned out to be an excellent choice.

In a one-design class, the boat's construction is strictly controlled; all boats must be identical in virtually all respects. Hulls, for example, must come from the same mold, only sails from authorized sailmakers are allowed, rigging must be identical, and so on. No modifications are allowed. The objective in the one-design classes is to eliminate any superiority gained by individual boat construction or hardware. It's skipper against skipper. The AMYA has several one-design racing classes.

The Victor Soling is an excellent choice for a group of neophyte racing skippers. It qualifies for the U. S. One Meter class, and it also can be sailed as a one-design club class. Either way, if it is built stock, it's a fast boat and easy to sail and handle. Have new skippers build the stock Soling kit; permit no changes unless all the skippers agree to the change. That change

is then made to all boats. The class uses the sails that come with the kit, and they all use the same sail winch, too. Both the Futaba S-25 proportional and Victor nonproportional winches work in this boat, but the Victor winch is quite a bit heavier. An Airtronic winch also works well. (See Chapter 7.)

Complete with sail winch and two-channel radio, you can race the Soling for under $200. Given the right set of weather conditions, it is competitive with other U. S. One Meter boats. Victor also has U. S. One Meter class semi-scale kits of the Stars and Stripes and Australia II available; but in my opinion their performance is not up to the Soling.

RACING: AN INTRODUCTION

The AMYA has a starting cassette with a one-minute countdown to the starting bell. All skippers keep their boats behind the starting line during the countdown, because the objective is to put your bow on the line just as the bell sounds.

During the countdown, each skipper tries to stake off a little piece of

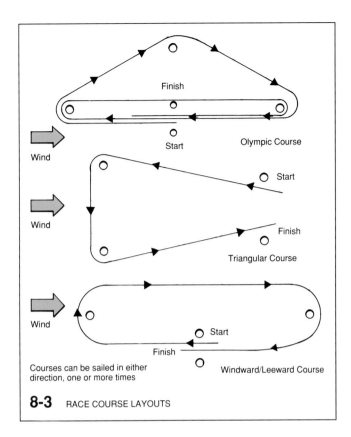

8-3 RACE COURSE LAYOUTS

Finish

Start

Olympic Course

Wind

Start

Finish

Triangular Course

Wind

Start

Finish

Windward/Leeward Course

Wind

Courses can be sailed in either
direction, one or more times

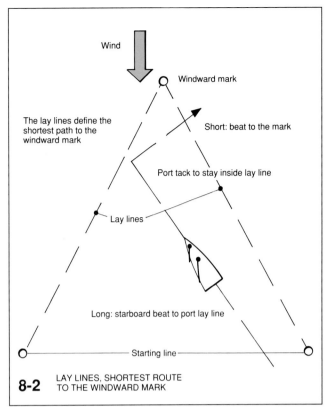

8-2 LAY LINES, SHORTEST ROUTE
TO THE WINDWARD MARK

Wind

Windward mark

The lay lines define the
shortest path to the
windward mark

Short: beat to the mark

Port tack to stay inside lay line

Lay lines

Long: starboard beat to port lay line

Starting line

the line as they maintain an air of forced calm. No one wants to telegraph their starting strategy. This is a nervous time for the skippers as each one tries to find the best lay line to the first mark. Crossing before the bell sounds is forbidden; the overanxious skipper must recross the line and start over. Since races are easily won or lost at the start, it is crucial not to cross early.

Wind shifts, a bad tack or gybe at the wrong instant, right-of-way loss, stalling as the bell sounds: these are things that mess up a good start. It takes plenty of concentration and attention to your boat to consistently start in the first three boats.

Each skipper assesses how long it takes his or her boat to cover the distance to the line. Should the boat be tacked or gybed? Can the boat accelerate in time to cross the line at the bell? Starts curl your toes with excitement! As the boat crosses the line, it should be at top speed or at least be accelerating to the windward mark. One of the best ways to do this is to lay back and time your approach while simultaneously observing the rules of the road. And don't forget to find the best lay line to the first mark, establish your place on the line, and listen to the starting tape. It's challenging and lots of fun!

It's precisely this challenge that transforms model sailboat racing from a hobby to a sport. Years ago, there was a raging dispute in the R/C frater-

nity over the builder of the model rule. R/C scale and aerobatic aircraft pilots were not allowed to compete in national competitions if they had not built the model they would fly in the competition. Today, it's perfectly acceptable to buy a ready-to-fly model aircraft and compete in a number of events. The pilot may be more of a sportsman than a hobbyist. In R/C sailboat racing, it is also permissible to race without having built the boat.

There is a strong sense of camaraderie that naturally develops in a group of skippers that has raced together for some time. Even if someone does something dumb that may reduce the chance of another skipper's winning a heat, strong words are rarely exchanged. Winning is great, but there is always another day; the overriding objective is to have fun.

THE RACING CLASSES

Years ago, the AMYA assumed the responsibility of registering and controlling all active racing classes. The class secretaries handle boat registrations, assign sail numbers, and maintain an active list of skippers racing in that class. They also schedule AMYA-sanctioned regional and national racing events for their class and publish class notes in the quarterly issues of *Model Yachting*.

Regattas for the various classes are held all over the country, and skippers often drive several hundred miles to participate in a weekend race series.

Some of the more popular classes draw hundreds of boats for two jam-packed days of racing. Heats are set up using a frequency matrix to ensure that each skipper races an equal number of times against every other skipper.

The AMYA requires a minimum of twenty registered boats to create a new racing class. If the number falls below twenty, it is dropped. Over the years, several classes have come and gone while others have mushroomed into large classes. The two most active classes at this time are the Marblehead and U. S. One Meter classes. There are thousands of these boats registered with the AMYA, but no one is really sure how many others are out there that are not registered.

The Marblehead class rules specify a maximum hull length of 50 inches and 800-square inches of sail. The U. S. One Meter class rules specify a hull length of 39-3/8 inches and 600-square inches of sail.

The popularity of these two classes is due to their ease of transport and outstanding performance in all types of weather. Both classes offer great speed and superb response. Neither class is considered to be a one design class. The U. S. One Meter class was developed as a low-cost alternative using balsa-planked hulls and homemade sails. Today, there are quite a few Kevlar and fiberglass hulls, but there are also plenty of winning wood hulls, too.

Both commercially-made and home-

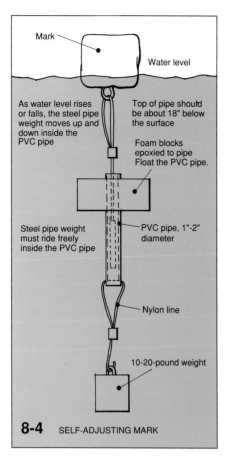

Mark

Water level

As water level rises or falls, the steel pipe weight moves up and down inside the PVC pipe

Top of pipe should be about 18" below the surface

Foam blocks epoxied to pipe Float the PVC pipe.

Steel pipe weight must ride freely inside the PVC pipe

PVC pipe, 1"-2" diameter

Nylon line

10-20-pound weight

8-4 SELF-ADJUSTING MARK

made sails are used on the U. S. One Meter. A careful builder still turns out a competitive boat going all the way from scratch. The founding class secretary, Bob Debow, has compiled a lengthy set of instructions and a long list of designs and construction plans; all are available for the cost of running copies. Bob has done an outstanding job of promoting this class and in no small way has been and still is responsible for the class' explosive growth.

The Marblehead class is the single largest AMYA class and leans more toward purchased components including hulls, sails, and spars. It is difficult for a beginner to construct a competitive Marblehead in the basement, and the class promoters make no bones about it. They suggest that the easiest way to race Marbleheads is to buy finished components (hull, spars, sails, winch, etc.) or a complete boat. Components and complete boats are generally for sale in the Marblehead clubs.

Both classes are open-design; that is, as long as the basic hull and sail measurements are met, the skipper can use any materials, hull shape, sails, and radio gear that he chooses to. This has encouraged the use of experimental materials like Kevlar, carbon fiber and light-machined and extruded aluminum components that increase strength and reduce weight. A lot of research has been done on lead

bulb and fin shapes. Rotating mast rigs are the latest wrinkle in Marblehead racing and are already having an effect on racing outcomes.

Geographically, you may find a particular class being raced in one part of the country and nowhere else. For example, the 36/600 Multihull class is confined to the San Diego area, which is its birthplace. Marbleheads are raced all over the country, but you only see U. S. One Meters in certain locales. Some classes focus on one coast or the other. So, you have to see for yourself what class, if any, is raced in your area. Your local hobby shop often can tell you where the racing scene is and who to contact.

The AMYA wrote and continues to modify the rules for each racing class. Each class secretary is responsible for polling the class members regarding pending rule changes. The rules, which are sometimes very specific and detailed, are meant to ensure that all boats in a regatta are essentially the same.

When you join the AMYA, you receive a bulky packet containing the racing rules, all active class rules, and the latest copy of *Model Yachting*. Model Yachting is filled with building and racing how-to-do-it material, racing results, scheduled regattas, and class news. The magazine alone is worth the price of membership. (See Chapter 2 for membership information.)

Following is a list of active AMYA racing classes. Note that the list changes from time to time as classes mature and are replaced. In each issue, *Model Yachting* lists the active classes along with class secretaries and their addresses and phone numbers. Some of the class secretaries can provide plans, kits, and complete boat sources along with the regatta schedules for their class. They all can tell you who is racing their class in your area.

AMYA Racing Classes (O/D = One-Design class):
• AC class
• East Coast 12 Meter
• Infinity 54 (O/D)
• "J" Boat
• Marblehead
• Newport 12 O/D
• Santa Barbara O/D
• Soling O/D
• Star 45
• U. S. One Meter
• 10 Rater
• 36/600
• 36/600 Multi-hull
• g-Forse 12 Meter

SIMPLIFIED RACING RULES

In the world of full-size sailboat racing, the rule book is governed by

the North American Yacht Racing Union (NAYRU). The rule book is incredibly lengthy with a bewildering set of complex rules intended to cover any situation that could happen at sea. In the case of full-size boats, it's understandable that the rulebook tries to cover every possible type of violation considering sailing's competitive nature and the amounts of time and money spent on racing. A dispute may end up in a court of law, if the rule book is not crystal clear, as in the recent case of the America's Cup boats.

However, in the R/C model boating world, things are quite a bit simpler; and we aim to keep it that way. The basic tenets in model sailboat racing are: 1) don't hit or otherwise slow the other boat if that boat has the right of way; 2) steer your boat to the correct side of the marks as you round them; and 3) the most important rule, of course, is have fun!

In terms of hitting or slowing, there are a few rules of the road that every skipper needs to know in order to prevent a race from turning into aquatic bumper-cars. Our club started racing several years ago. At the time, we decided to start racing with virtually no rules and to see what rules evolved. In a short time, it was obvious that we had to implement some basic right-of-way rules in order to eliminate the hull banging at the starting line and marks. No one was sure who had the right of way, who had to yield, and, of course, we all wanted to win! Even the finish line became a point of contention.

Model sailboat collisions can be fatal. Some hulls are lightly built, and a good bump from the bow of another boat can hole the hull and literally sink it. Right-of-way rules eliminate this scenario. Mandatory soft bumpers on the bow of each boat also help. Following is a list of the rules adopted by our club. Feel free to edit as necessary to fit your regattas. Our rules were adapted in simplified form from the AMYA rule book. The rules are illustrated in figure 8-1.

SIMPLIFIED RIGHT-OF-WAY RULES

1) A boat on port tack always yields to a boat on starboard tack. (See figure 8-1A.)

2) When one boat overtakes the boat in front of it, the overtaking boat stays in the clear. The boat being overtaken always has the right of way.

3) When two boats are running side-by-side, the boat to leeward has the right of way over the windward boat.

4) A boat that is tacking or gybing always stays clear of boats that are

Fig. 8-5A. A good start! Six AMYA Marblehead class boats charge to the windward mark in heavy air.

still sailing.

5) When two boats approach a mark, if the inside boat is overlapping the outside boat and is within two boat lengths of the mark, the outside boat yields and gives the inside boat adequate room to round the mark.

6) When a boat is doing a penalty turn or restarting, it never has the right of way.

SCORING

For several years, our club has used the AMYA scoring method. It's a reverse scoring method where the objective is to garner as few points as possible over the day and, ultimately, the season. The winner of each heat gets 3/4 point, the second place gets two points, third place gets three points, fourth gets four points and so on. Boats that entered but did not start for equipment reasons or whatever receive a Did Not Start (DNS),

Fig. 8-5B. It only takes two boats to race. Here two Marbleheads round the windward mark. Note both boats have their sails sheeted in hard as they beat to windward.

Fig. 8-6. A Marblehead class skipper gets set to retrieve his boat. Note his rubber boots; they are useful when launching or retrieving your boat.

Fig. 8-7. It's always handy to have a retrieval tug to rescue sailboats that have stalled while racing. This tug pulls a 20-foot length of nylon rope with a big float at the end of the line. To retrieve a sailboat, the tug circles the dead boat until the nylon rope is wrapped around the keel fin. It's then towed back to shore.

which is two points plus the number of boats that did finish the heat. If a boat does not finish a heat it started due to equipment failure, that boat receives a Did Not Finish (DNF). One point is added to your score plus the number of boats that did finish. If you are unlucky enough to foul someone, you have four points added to your heat score.

A typical race day usually consists of anywhere from six to fifteen races. Most clubs start the first race at about 10:00 A.M. and the last by 2:00 P.M. Someone has to record the standings for each heat and total up the scores for the day. It's a good idea to have one or two throw-away days so that no skipper is unduly penalized at the end of the season because he missed a couple of race days. The highest scores are thrown out and this tends to even things out a bit. But the bottom line is if you want to keep your accrued score low, be at the pond just about every race day. The DNS scores are the fastest way to drop in the overall standings.

STARTING THE RACE

Unlike cars or race horses, sailboats are not put in a straight line and simultaneously released at a given signal. They are in the water and sailing before the start of the race and they cross the imaginary starting line just as the bell or cannon sounds. Crossing the line before the starting signal means the skipper must sail back across the line and do a restart. If this happens seconds before the gun goes off, it's a sure bet that skipper is already in trouble and hasn't even started yet!

The winning skipper knows his boat so well that he consistently hits the line right at the bell. This kind of start wins races; you must strive to be first or one of the first boats across the line. Going across as the third or fourth boat puts you at a severe disadvantage because you already are playing catch up when the objective is to get out in front and stay there. You must practice starts if you want to be a winning skipper!

Windward starts are the order of each race day. When our club started, it always did not use this rule. We started upwind, downwind, and with the wind on the beam. It didn't take long to figure out why boats are always started into the wind. When we started on a downwind run or reach, the boats went so fast across the line that sometimes skippers could not react fast enough to avoid collisions. On windy days, we left the pond with paint scars all over our hulls from the various starting line altercations.

Someone finally suggested that we could eliminate such awesome boat speeds in confined quarters if we simply used windward starts! By adopting this, we reduced greatly the number of accidental rammings and failures to yield right of way. This rule makes a lot of sense, particularly if you are sailing with beginning skippers.

The AMYA one-minute starting tape provides an audible, graduated one-minute countdown. Each skipper tries to hit the imaginary starting line just as the bell rings for the start. The better skippers seem to lay back, out of harms way, and in relatively clean air. This gives them room to accelerate and yield, if required, as they drive to the line.

A boat on starboard tack has the right of way over a boat on port tack. At the start, many skippers use starboard tack to claim right of way. However, it is to your advantage at times to put your boat on port tack if it gives you a faster lay line to the windward mark. It depends, too, on where your boat is located behind the line with respect to the windward mark.

Sometimes in light air it's difficult to know what tack to take across the line. One way to determine this is to beat on either tack up to the line. At the line, turn the boat directly into the wind (luffing up). The sails flap uselessly for a few seconds; but eventually the boat falls off on one tack or the other. Try this a couple of times; whichever way it wants to go is the tack you take to the windward mark.

As shown in figure 8-2, you also can draw two imaginary lines from the two ends of the starting line to the windward mark. These are the lay lines to that mark, and you do all your sailing within these lines. If you go outside these lines, you go much further than is necessary to get to the mark. The shortest path to the mark is between these lines.

UNDERWAY AND RACING

Once across the line, you stay on the tack you began for as long as possible. Make the first leg to the mark the longest leg. In other words, don't sail fifteen feet past the starting line and go over on the other tack. This approach leaves you sufficient maneuvering room as you approach the mark so that if you do run into a wind shift or stoppage at the mark, you sail a short rather than a long leg to get out of it. Long leg to short leg helps you keep your options open. The same strategy is used for every mark, not just the first.

On light air days, another effective tactic is to do what the old salts call "taking a header." When beating to windward, the boat may slow down or stop. The sails flap, you stall, and another boat twenty feet away sails right by. Very frustrating. You sailed your boat into a wind shear (the other skipper missed it), a point where the wind abruptly changes direction. If you had been paying attention, chances are you would have seen it coming.

The alert skipper always is watching for signs of boat slowing and sail luffing (flapping); they are sure signs that the boat is approaching a shear. To get out of this problem, the rudder is used to bring the boat to the other tack. In some instances, the boat wants to switch tacks without rudder input; let it. Beginners fight this tendency and try to keep their boat on the present tack. Experience helps you see the shears coming, and you know when to let the boat take the header and put itself on the opposite tack. The net result is that you maintain boat speed. You may have to sail a longer course, but speed offsets the longer distance. You get there faster than the skipper who didn't take the header.

PENALTY TURNS

If a skipper violates a rule, penalty turns are incurred. For example, if a skipper turns inside a mark, he goes back and re-rounds the mark by making one or more 360-degree turns around the mark. Failure to yield the right of way, forcing an inside boat at the mark into the mark, and so on, requires the errant skipper to execute the penalty turns.

Some clubs assign this task to a nonparticipating skipper, (one who is familiar with the rules). Other clubs use the honor system. When a skipper thinks a foul has occurred, he immediately says so; the rules person agrees or disagrees. If agreed to, the guilty skipper does the required penalty turns. Protests also are lodged and settled after the race is over.

THE RACE COURSE

The course is virtually any shape that allows windward starting. When starting into the wind, the boats move relatively slowly and are managed easier than if they started on a run or reach. It's also a much better test of skipper skills. Anyone can steer a boat downwind—it takes skill and practice to sail into the wind.

Fig. 8-8A. AMYA class 10 Rater. These are relatively large heavy boats that handle and perform much like real boats, particularly in heavy air. Due to their size, it is not a large racing class.

Figure 8-3 shows several layouts that work. Depending on wind speed, distance between the marks, and the skill levels, you use any pattern of marks to round, as long as there is a windward (into the wind) leg, a reaching (wind on the beam) leg, and a running leg (wind behind the boat). This course tests the skill of each skipper to sail on all points of sail. It also eliminates the advantage one boat has over another: for example, one boat is much faster downwind than the others but slower going to windward. Twice around the course is a good rule of thumb on a windy day, and once around if the wind is light. Marks should be 100 to 200 feet apart.

If possible, the rectangular or triangular course is preferred over the out-and-back course. The rectangular and triangular courses force each skipper to sail on all three basic points of sail, whereas the out-and-back course only uses two of the three. Also, the out-and-back course cannot be rerouted to allow for wind shifts. It's a good idea to have five or six marks set, and use any three to get the windward, reaching, and running course. One of the three marks is used as the far end of the starting line. A portable mark, with a weight and retrieval line attached, can be thrown from shore to establish the near end of the starting line.

A two-mark starting line clearly defines the imaginary starting line and gives the skippers a good sight line from shore to make sure they don't cross early. For anything but a two-boat start, the distance between

Fig. 8-8B. AMYA class U.S. One Meter. One of the hottest and fastest growing racing classes, these boats are quick and will fit assembled in a mid-size station wagon.

the two starting marks should be at least 20 feet apart.

Typical heats run five to ten minutes. The AMYA rules suggest a five-minute interval between heats. If a boat isn't ready to go in that time, then it receives a Did Not Start (DNS) for the next heat.

MARKS

Marks are made easily from any waterproof, buoyant material. If you place them way out on the pond, make them highly visible by all means. On a bright, sunny day, mark visibility can be severely reduced by the glare and sparkle of the sun on the water. High-visibility day-glo orange boat fenders work fine; so do one-gallon milk jugs if you can keep them painted.

Painting the inside of the jug might work. Plywood and construction insulating foam material also can be used,

but make sure they are anchored adequately to the pond bottom. Figure 8-4 shows how our club devised a method to let the marks rise and fall during the summer as the pond level changed. And make your marks geese and duck proof. The local geese community has pecked ours quite heavily.

RACING TACTICS

The winning skipper knows his boat. It takes lots of practice to instinctively know what the boat does in a given set of wind conditions. The boat is trimmed properly for the weather that day, and lee or weather helm is eliminated so the skipper is not using excessive rudder. Clew outhauls are matched to the weather, along with the backstay tension. The time to learn how to do this is on those weekends when there is no racing.

The skipper must be comfortable

controlling the boat. For example, when the boat is coming straight at the skipper, rudder control is reversed. Left is right and right is left. Stick control must be instinctive. And with practice it will happen.

Hit the line when the bell rings. It looks easy: a bunch of boats casually cruising as the one-minute tape counts down. In reality, it is difficult. Because of the proximity of the other boats, you might have your air stolen at the last second, you might have to yield to a starboard tack, or you might even hit the line early. The best advice at the start is: 1) Stay in clear air and 2) lay back so the boat can accelerate as it approaches the starting line (figure 8-5A).

Luff up to the line to determine the best tack to the windward mark.

Starboard tack has the right of way. Everything else being equal, it is a good idea to get on starboard tack (wind on the starboard side of the boat) before you cross the starting line. That way, any boat that threatens your path on port tack, yields as you call for right of way. However, sailboat racing being as unpredictable as it is, there may be a better opportunity or shorter route to the windward mark by putting the boat on port tack and being ready to yield, if necessary, to a boat on starboard tack.

This same tactic is used if you and another skipper engage in a tacking duel to the windward mark. If both boats are in the clear and one of them is on starboard tack, the other yields. Done properly, it gets you to the first mark a length or two before the other boat (figure 8-5B).

Use the rudder sparingly. Use sail trim to keep the boat on the line to the next mark. You put your boat at a serious disadvantage if your boat has so much weather helm that you need rudder. To reduce weather helm, rake the mast forward. In gross cases, restep the entire mast forward. Moving the jib forward also helps. Do the opposite to increase weather helm. Keep in mind that the trim used to correct weather helm is only good for the wind conditions on the day you do it. Plan on doing this every time you go to the pond.

If the boat is trimmed properly, it should sail all three legs (windward, reaching, and running) with a minimum of rudder. Trim the boat to sail as if it's on rails. It can be done; that's why there are so many adjustments on a sailboat.

Stay in clear air. When I started racing, I thought it was neat to chase the other guy, to stay right behind him or try to get on the inside, like track racing. In sailboat racing, however, the wind and its shifts are crucial fac-

Fig. 8-8C. AMYA class Marblehead. An open class, these boats are one of the fastest and most popular classes. They are extremely fast and feature high tech components.

Fig. 8-8D. Victor Manufacturing's Soling qualifies for U.S. One Meter class. Many clubs use this kit as a club one design. It is unbeatable on all scores as a beginner's boat. Built per the kit's excellent instructions and kept light, it will compete with the AMYA stable of U.S. One Meter designs.

tors. We need the wind to maintain heading and speed, and crowding other boats defeats the ability of the wind to do its job. So, stay in the clear.

Sometimes, it's actually faster to sail a longer route to the mark, staying clear of the fleet. If you do get close, always stay to the windward side of the boat you are trying to pass. This blanks or steals his wind and slows him down while you slingshot past him. This is a very effective tactic. By staying to windward, you put the other boat in your wind shadow. Think of the wind as the sun; you block his sunlight. Conversely, stay out of the other boats' wind shadows!

Maintain way and minimize tacks. Maintaining way is the nautical term for keeeping your boat moving at all times. You reduce way if you sail too close to the wind, do not fully extend your sails when running downwind, make violent turns, or have bad sail trim. Keeping your speed up requires a lot of concentration from the skipper. Top skippers constantly retrim the sails to maximize sail lift and boat speed.

If the unwary skipper "pinches" and consequently stalls the boat going to windward, that race is probably lost before the boat crosses the line, particularly at the start in light air. It may take several seconds or more to get the stalled boat moving again. By then, the fleet is long gone on their way to the windward mark! Trim sails carefully and thoughtfully when the breeze is light.

There are no hard and fast rules about when to tack; but as a general rule of thumb, avoid tacking until you are almost to the mark. In other words, make the first leg to the mark as long as possible before you tack. Avoid tacking like the plague; every tack slows the boat and gives other boats the chance to move up.

Sail tune and trim. This is vitally important to maximizing boat speed. Reducing weather helm was covered already. The boom vang (the tensioner between the main boom and the bottom of the mast) also needs frequent trim. It should be tightened in heavy air and loosened in light air.

If your boat has a servo-tensioned backstay adjuster, tension the backstay going to windward and slack it running downwind. Backstay tension tightens the jibstay and flattens the jib, which improves the jib's windward performance. Slacking the backstay loosens the jibstay and allows the jib to efficiently belly out somewhat when running downwind

Most boats don't have servo-adjusted backstays, so they are manually adjusted on shore. Tighten it in heavy air, and loosen in light air. Working in concert with the jibstay, the jib should be flatter in heavy air than in light air. The backstay also controls the effort required to swing the jib in and out. When running downwind, it's very important that the jib be swung out as far as it can go. If it is not coming out all the way, try slacking the backstay a bit.

Make the main and jib clew outhauls more taut in heavy air than in light air. In other words, the main and jib are flattened in heavy air and full in light air. A good starting point is to set the clew outhauls so that you can just get a finger between the boom and the sail foot. Tighten or loosen from there.

The jib sheet must allow the jib to swing out past the 90-degree point when running downwind. If you let the jib go past the point of perpendicularity, it will remain extended in very light air. The main sail, of course, goes out to the side shrouds. With the sails closehauled, both jib and main are right over the deck. In light air, ease the sheets a bit when closehauled.

The jib always is set a few degrees further out than the main to ensure an effective slot is maintained between the jib and main. The jib is never pulled in further than the main.

Remember, none of the racing rules is cast in bronze. You can set up your first regatta any way you like. From our experience, it's probably better to start with very few or even no rules with a bunch of new skippers. Except no one starts early without having to recross the line.

Fig. 9-1. A 48-inch replica of the International One Design. These boats still race in Long Island Sound and Bermuda. Just like the real boat, the model is slow to answer the rudder. It's very pretty under sail.

Fig. 9-2. Another classic wooden boat, John Alden's Malabar Jr. shown here with Bermuda sail plan. This boat is a joy to sail. The hull length with boom and boomkin is 48 inches. The sails are cut from spinnaker cloth.

9

SCALE SAILBOATS

Many of us prefer the challenge of designing, building, and sailing scale or semi-scale sailboats (figure 9-1). Just about every type of real sailboat has been replicated in miniature and successfully launched and sailed. All it takes is enough interest to research the hull station lines and sail plan. Chapter 4 outlines the necessary steps to blow up scale drawings to the desired size.

If you are not a scratchbuilder, Robbe has several semi-scale kits that sail very well. These are well-designed and easy-to-build kits that sail very well.

Scale models of sloops, ketches,

yawls, even square-rigged, barks, and brigantines have been built and sailed. It's a wonderful way to explore full-size ship history, design, and construction. Some modelers specialize in a particular ship genre. An example is American sailing ships of the nineteenth century. If you enjoy recreating nautical history, building and sailing replicas is a great way to enhance and implement your hobby (figure 9-2).

As an example; what if two early America's Cup boats were built to the same scale and then match raced? Do the models replicate their full-size counterparts' relative performances? They should be close if the two boats

are built in the same way. And don't forget their visual appeal on the water, both boats racing to windward, lee rail down and driving hard. The choice is yours: from junks to trimarans and everything in between.

Some model skippers believe that scale boats simply don't sail well. I feel qualified to dispute that claim, having built several exact-scale boats myself and having observed others' efforts. Scale boats can and do sail very well. No, they are not as fast as their non-scale racing sisters. But that's not why we build them. Their beauty under sail and their historical or aesthetic appeal outweigh any speed disadvantage. They are a handful to sail in heavy air; but if sailing is done only when the wind is less than 10 to 12 miles per hour, scale boats provide plenty of excitement, satisfaction, and pleasure at the pond. (They will also draw quite a crowd.)

SIZE, SAIL AREA, AND KEELS

The minimum model hull length is about 30 inches. Anything less than 30 inches causes problems when trying to install the receiver and sail winch. The boat will be difficult to sail, very tipsy, and twitchy on the rudder. A 30-inch hull is able to handle sail plans up to 500 square inches. By comparison, a 48-inch hull handles 900 squares without having to shorten the mast height. A 72-inch hull can carry 1,500 square inches of sail.

Keel depth is a major factor in determining the overall stiffness of the boat. (That is how easy it is for the wind to heel the boat.) The deeper the keel, the taller the sail rig can be. A scale keel can be deepened and, in some cases, is on the model. The out-of-scale keel is not seen when the boat is sailing; it significantly improves windward performance, allowing the skipper to point higher than with the scale keel. The scale keel can be deepened 40 to 50 percent; but make sure that the center of gravity is not changed when the keel is deepened.

The beam of the model is very important; it works in conjunction with the keel to provide the hull's righting moment (figure 9-3). The typical racing hull has a very deep fin and bulb keel that provides adequate stiffness even in heavy air. With its shallower keel, the scale boat relies less on the keel and more on its beam for stiffness. For this reason, it's a good idea to select a scale boat with a moderate to wide beam. The wider beam improves stiffness in strong breezes and keeps the water out of the cabin when driving hard to windward. Since most full-size boats tend to be much beamier than the AMYA-type racing hulls, it isn't a problem to find suitable subjects. The wider beam also simplifies the radio board installation. There is plenty of room to swing the sail winch output arm (figure 9-4).

CONSTRUCTION

Select a design and determine how big it's going to be. Before construction starts, have the receiver, battery pack, and sail winch on hand to see how everything is going to fit into the hull. Lay the components right on a full-size sketch of the top and side views of the hull to make sure everything fits. Be sure to position the components low in the hull to keep the center of gravity as low as possible.

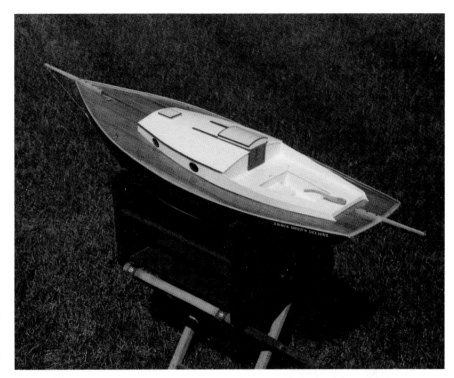

Fig. 9-3. Malabar Jr. with her mast removed. The deck is planked with mahogany.

Fig. 9-4. John Alden's Malabar Jr. with a gaff-sail rig. This version sailed poorly to windward and answered the rudder slowly.

Fig. 9-5. Sloop versus ketch. On the left is the Phil Rhodes double-ended ketch Dogstar. Chasing it on the right is John Alden's Malabar Jr. In this case they are evenly matched for speed, but the ketch is faster to windward.

Check for clearance problems associated with the frames, mast support posts (one under each mast running down to the keelson), the rudder pushrod/cables, and the like. Lay these items out while the model is still on paper. Planning at this stage saves many headaches later.

Make sketches to determine where the hatches are located and how they integrate into the deck or cabin structure. From below decks out to the booms, sheet routings have to take the hatch locations into account. The sheets should never exit through removable hatch covers. Try to build the model in your head before you ever cut any wood. Rudder installations cause some head scratching because the rudders often are hung right on the stern of the boat, unlike the racing hulls where the rudder post goes up through the hull. The simplest method is a rigid dowel or music wire pushrod running from the rudder servo to the rudder horn. However, there are cases where this does not work. Case in point is my double-ender ketch where I had to run fishing leader cables from the rudder servo out through hull eyelets to a control horn mounted on the rudder. There was no way a rigid

pushrod could be snaked through the maze in the stern, including the mizzen sail sheet and guides and extremely cramped quarters due to the canoe stern. At the same time, I had to make sure the rudder cables did not interfere with the sail winch output arm and main sail sheet.

A full-depth scale cockpit prevents you from running a straight pushrod from the rudder servo to the rudder horn. In these instances, right-angle aileron bellcranks solve the problem. Flexible pushrods also are used. Both items are available at any well-stocked R/C aircraft hobby counter. While you're there, be sure to see what other fittings are available, such as nylon and steel clevises and ball-joint connectors.

Plan the keel attachment method well ahead since it directly influences the type of keelson you use. If the hull is wood framed with a pine or spruce keelson, the lead keel with it's cast-in bolts is bolted directly through the keelson with suitable reinforcement built in around the attach bolts. An alternate method is to plank the keel when you plank the hull, and then pour lead birdshot into the hollow keel cavity until the hull floats on its lines.

Completely fiberglass balsa-planked hulls on the outside with 3- to 6-ounce cloth to strengthen the hull skin and reinforce the keel area. Don't bother with a removable keel. It sounds like a good idea, but it's unlikely that it has to be removed.

Keelsons are at least 1/4-inch by 1/2-inch pine or spruce, but 3/8-inch by 5/8-inch are better. The keelson is laminated from a couple of strips to gain more strength and to ease the bending strain. Where the keel bolts come through the hull, strips are glued to both sides of the keelson to spread out the keel load. If the keel skin is planked up as an integral part of the hull skin, use 1/4-inch square pine as the internal keel outline on the bottom of the boat. The lead shot rests on this pine. For the person with no lead casting experience, lead birdshot and epoxy are an excellent alternative to a poured lead keel.

The easiest and most inexpensive way to scratchbuild a scale boat hull is to use the time-honored method of plywood frames, balsa planking, and fiberglass skin. Unlike the racing hulls with temporary frames, the frames in a scale boat are left in. This method of construction is described in detail in

Fig. 9-6. The Malabar Jr. and Dogstar beat to windward—a pretty sight indeed. Sailing to windward, the scale boats cannot be sheeted in as hard as their racing cousins. These boats are more tender and will heel excessively if they are sheeted in hard.

Chapter 4 (figure 9-7).

Spars are aluminum or wood in keeping with the original boat. Use wood if you build a 1920s gaff-rigged sloop; but if you build a modern vessel, then aluminum spars from Pop-Up are appropriate. Sails made in the conventional fashion are described in Chapter 6. If its an older boat, a nice touch is to attach or bend on the sails using proto-typical wood hoops.

It's very important to keep the center of gravity as low as possible. Locate all components in the widest, deepest part of the hull. This preserves the balance and maximizes installation room.

RACING

Yes, you can race scale boats (figure 9-5). More than one club schedules and runs scale regattas where the unmatched boats are rated on a handicap system so each boat has a fair shot at winning. On the other end of the scale, another club uses a one-design approach with all hulls coming from the same kit, mold, or set of shadows. Still another club races Friendship sloops, all built from the Laughing Whale kit (figure 9-6).

Whether you prefer to race or go it alone, there is no longer any reason not to pursue your dream if you like scale. Scale sailing is fun, realistic, and opens up a whole new world of R/C sailing to beginners, racing skippers, nautical historians, and even static display boat builders who want to see their mantelpiece creation take to the water.

Fig. 9-7. The Dogstar double-ended ketch hull still on the building board. Its balsa planked hull has been covered with six-ounce fiberglass and epoxy resin.

GLOSSARY OF SAILING TERMS

To the neophyte skipper it may seem as if the crew at the pond is speaking another language when they start talking boats. And well they are. The language of sailing vessels is rich with centuries of tradition. You owe it to yourself to study this glossary. In no time you'll be talking like an old salt.

Backstay: An adjustable line that supports the mast. It runs from the transom of the hull to the masthead crane or jenny strut.

Batten: Thin wood or plastic strips attached to the back half of the sails. They impart needed stiffness and flatten the latter half of the sail.

To Beat: To sail a course into the wind within ninety to forty-five degrees of the direction of the wind.

Bow: Front of the boat.

Chain Plates: Stainless steel or brass deck fittings to which the side shrouds are attached.

Clew: The bottom corner of a sail at its trailing edge.

Clew outhaul: An adjustable line running from the clew of the sail to the end of the boom. It's used to slacken or tighten the foot of the sail.

Fair: A smooth curve with no bumps or depressions. A hull is said to be fair.

Fairlead: The exit point through the hull for a main or jib sheet.

Fin: A narrow vertical fin that extends below the water line. Acts as a vertical stabilizer, minimizing side-wise motion or leeway when the boat is underway.

Foot: The bottom edge of the sail.

Forestay: An adjustable line running from the bow or bowsprit to the top of the mast (masthead). Seldom used on non-scale model racing yachts. In this case the jibstay performs the same function.

Gooseneck: A flexible hinged fitting which securely retains the main boom to the mast.

Halyard: A line used to raise or lower a sail. Seldom used on model yachts.

Harden: To tightly sheet in the sails over the boat, allowing the boat to point higher into the wind.

Head: The very top corner of the sail.

Jib Rack: A model yacht deck fitting to which the jib boom or club is attached.

Jib Stay: An adjustable line running from the fore end of the jib club to either high up on the mast or the masthead. Functions in lieu of a forestay.

Jibe: To change direction while running downwind so as to shift the wind from one side of the boat to the other. An exciting maneuver, challenging in high winds.

Keelson: Laminated strips (usually spruce or pine in a model yacht) running the full length of the inside of the hull to stiffen it.

Leech: A straight line drawn from the head of the sail to its clew. Used in model yachting classes to determine maximum allowable sail area.

Leeway: Sideways motion a sailboat makes when the wind is not directly behind the boat. The fin or keel reduces this motion.

Luff: The leading edge of the sail, fastens to the mast or jib stay.

Luffing Up: To turn the boat straight into the wind or slacken the sheets. Either maneuver slows or stops the boat, while the sails flap uselessly.

Mast Step: A deck fitting which locates the mast in one of two or three positions.

Port: The left side of the boat while facing forward.

Reach: Sailing on a line from approximately 90 to 140 degrees of the wind.

Roach: A curved line running from the clew to the head of the sail. Defines the maximum allowable sail area for a racing class.

Run: Sailing on a line from approximately 140 to 180 degrees of the wind.

Shadows: Temporary frames used only during hull planking.

Sheer Clamps: Laminated stringers which define the outline of the deck and stiffen the deck-to-hull attachment.

Sheet: Lines running from the sail control unit inside the hull through fairleads and out to the main and jib booms. Used to control sail settings.

Starboard: The right side of the boat while facing forward.

Tack: 1) The bottom corner of a sail at its leading edge. 2) To change direction of the boat so as to put the wind on the opposite side of the boat, for example , to switch from port to starboard tack.

Vang: An adjustable and sturdy line running from the main boom to the bottom of the mast. It prevents the boom from lifting and ballooning the main sail as it is eased out before the wind.

Water Line: A real or imaginary line on the hull at which the boat should float when fully ballasted and ready to sail.